SLEEPING POLICEMEN

Sleeping Policemen is the result of an exciting and innovative collaboration between playwrights Howard Brenton and Tunde Ikoli, and director Roland Rees. Commissioned by Foco Novo, the brief was for each writer to create a play set in Peckham in 1983, using the same six characters but written from his own point of view. Following a series of regular meetings and finally a workshop with six actors, they separated, each to write his own play. When the scripts were complete, the writers met again and, together with the director, intercut them into one play.

'The result is like a radicalised, phantasmagoric *Under Milk Wood* . . . Next time I pass through or linger in Peckham I shall certainly look at the place with fresh eyes . . . for the play does quite effectively suggest that every block of council flats teems with eccentric human dramas.' Michael Billington, *Guardian*

'An impressionistic kaleidoscope of diverse daily wretchedness . . . haunting and evocative.' Martin Hoyle, *Financial Times*

D0144096

by Howard Brenton

THE CHURCHILL PLAY
EPSOM DOWNS
THE GENIUS
HITLER DANCES
MAGNIFICENCE
PLAYS FOR THE POOR THEATRE
(The Saliva Milkshake, Christie in Love, Gum and Goo, Heads,
    The Education of Skinny Spew)
REVENGE
THE ROMANS IN BRITAIN
SORE THROATS & SONNETS OF LOVE AND OPPOSITION
WEAPONS OF HAPPINESS

with David Hare

BRASSNECK

translation

THE LIFE OF GALILEO by Bertolt Brecht
DANTON'S DEATH by Georg Büchner

SLEEPING
POLICEMEN

HOWARD BRENTON
&
TUNDE IKOLI

A Methuen New Theatrescript
Methuen · London and New York

A METHUEN PAPERBACK

First published as a Methuen Paperback original in 1984 by Methuen London Ltd,
11 New Fetter Lane, London EC4P 4EE and
Methuen Inc, 733 Third Avenue, New York NY 10017, USA
Copyright © 1984 by Howard Brenton and Tunde Ikoli
Printed in Great Britain by Expression Printers Ltd, London N7

ISBN 0 413 55660 3

CAUTION
All rights whatsoever in this play are strictly reserved and application for performance etc,
should be made to Margaret Ramsay Ltd, 14a Goodwin's Court, St Martin's Lane,
London WC2N 4LL.

Introduction

Along the broad slopes of Peckham railway embankments the wildlife is doing fine: there are magpies and foxes, and domestic cats stalk field mice through the wild grasses. If you know which broken fence to go through in September, through which derelict garden, you can find blackberries in profusion. Kestrels can be seen hovering over the patches of tin-hoarded wasteland. It is extraordinary how in south London small trees, bushes, grasses and wild flowers flourish in unlikely corners, the odd vacant sites down backstreets that seem uncharted, even in the street maps of *London A – Z*. Nature will burst up through any crack in the concrete. Mind you, we must not be romantic about the Peckham landscape: hovering kestrels in the skies are not as common as the police helicopters which take in Peckham as they circle from dawn to dusk over Brixton, a few miles away – 'traffic helicopters' they say, though Peckham residents look up and have more sinister explanations for the endless aerial surveillance.

Bert Bloggs, the ragged-trousered poet in *Sleeping Policemen*, sees the citizens of Peckham as a lost army, temporarily encamped amongst the difficult terrain of decayed and cramped nineteenth-century terraces, scruffy parks and battered high-rise estates. Setting out at night with his two dogs, one named War, the other named Peace, he walks the streets at great speed to 'raise morale', like Henry the Fifth in Shakespeare's play touring the campfires before the battle of Agincourt. His view of the area is somewhat lurid, but then he is a poet and there is a sideways truth in what he says. Few living in Peckham were born there, they pass through or end up as citizens of Southwark, drifting on the unpredictable tides of housing policies in London. Dreams of moving away are frequent in conversations. Bert's 'vast human encampment of the Borough of Southwark' is not so much a demoralised army as a puzzled one, left behind in a war it only dimly remembers.

The sense of being passed by, of loss, of disinheritance, comes at you constantly in Peckham. But it does so in a fragmentary way: in the oddity of personal histories, the humour, in the sometimes hair-raising difficulties of the many action groups trying to get measures of self-help going, in the quirkiness of what people tell you about themselves. *Sleeping Policemen* was called 'expressionist' and 'dream-like' by some critics, but no – its stories and incidents are common. The wealth of strange human behaviour is inexhaustible in a poor, socially chaotic urban borough and often quite baffling. For example what 'sociological theory' can explain the local mania for keeping ducks as pets, often illegally in council flats? 'Can you look after my duck? My social worker's coming round.' One resident recently bought a small shetland pony, which lives happily in his garden: he explained 'Well, the kids wanted a video, but for thirty quid a shetland pony's a better buy anyway'. The old adage 'put it in a play and no one will believe you' is very true when writing about life in Peckham.

I hope *Sleeping Policemen*, as well as being a truthful entertainment, is an antidote to the glum stereo-type of the working class in the age of high unemployment. Peckhamites are not the shuffling figures that official statistics summon up, nor are they the ashen faces talking in close-up on grainy film about 'poverty 'n' violence' in the stock television documentaries. This is not to deny there is suffering. Under the pressure some do go down into mind-rotting lethargy, drunkeness, the destructive phantasmagoria of racism, and crime. The 'new poverty' of which Jeremy Seabrook writes with such a fine and powerful anger is everywhere (though even he is in danger of being seduced by the phoney grey imagery so attractive to literary minds when writing of social deprivation). *Sleeping Policemen* would have turned into one long horror story if it were made from the 'case loads' of workers in the social services. But the play would have then been a lie. 'Look at the way they want us to live' shouts Elizabeth Jones at the latest crisis in her life – her defiance and resistance, practical, womanly, undramatic, a day to day struggle, is as much part of the truth as the tales of domestic mayhem, racism and street violence. A cut line in the play, delivered with some irony to a middle class interloper, was 'People *are* living round here, y'know'.

Peckham lacks many things, but perhaps the greatest is a sense of unity. People live in thousands of tiny villages, some as small as a household: there is little awareness of the place as a whole, as a community. That is why *Sleeping Policemen* begins with a collage of soliloquies by people living alone or in their own heads. There is no local patriotism as there is in New York's Harlem, Brixton or Toxteth ('local patriotism' can, of course, be inverted! The hatred of an area can give a political awareness to its citizens.) 'How we divide, shy and frightened' says the saintly Castella Martin in the play.

An anecdote, from a Southwark Labour Councillor, illustrates this view of the area as many, tiny human islands. A small public garden was opened, intended for the people of a tower block one hundred yards away, but they ignored it; then the Council was approached by some of the resdidents of the block who said 'Can't we have a park like that? Near us?' A hundred yards from where you live is foreign territory in Peckham, nothing to do with you.

This 'apathy' is the bane of hard-working local socialists, trying to awaken some class consciousness. The meeting scene in part two of the play shows, with some affection, how wearing upon the activist's soul local action can be. But it is not apathy, it is part of the stress: people's energies are focused elsewhere. They concentrate on keeping the small flame of their own campfire alight, so great are the hassles. Faced with the discovery of dry rot in her council flat, Elizabeth Jones says 'One more thing go wrong and I could drown', a phrase that could be a Peckham anthem. The complexties of dealing with the housing authorities and the DHSS are all-engrossing, an endless playing of and being played by the system, a higher mathematics of everyday life that would stretch the financial acumen of a high Treasury official in Whitehall. How long would the present Chancellor of the Exchequer last, unemployed and living on the North Peckham Estate? Give him, what, six months to crack and be drinking his giro cheque away before his wife could get her hands on it? There are many brilliant people living in Peckham. They who keep their heads above water on the estates are Einsteins of daily life. That they have to be is a wrong that will take a social revolution to put to rights.

Howard Brenton

Director's Note

I founded Foco Novo amidst the explosion of new theatre in the late sixties and early seventies. It means 'new starting point' and was the title of our first production. As Artistic Director, it was my policy to collaborate with writers, actors and designers on projects. In many cases, I was instrumental in bringing a theme or story to a writer and the process started from there.

It is the policy of the Company to offer new work throughout the UK to audiences who would not normally have the opportunity to see such plays. To date the Company has produced 28 plays and has toured large theatres as well as miners' welfare halls and youth clubs. It has produced Brecht and Büchner and *The Elephant Man*, and now most recently *Sleeping Policemen*, about the undergrowth of life in Peckham. Whether we appear in a major theatre or in a youth club the same basic approach to the work and to the standard of presentation has been unwavering.

Sleeping Policemen is a response to living in an area rich with the potential of life but poor in the resources for life. The arena of local politics, its practice within and effect upon a specific neighbourhood, is an experience often by-passed.

Foco Novo commissioned Howard Brenton and Tunde Ikoli to write a play about Peckham. This was a capitalisation upon the work produced with *Sink or Swim* by Tunde Ikoli – about black and white youth – which the Company presented in Peckham during the summer of 1982.

The brief for the two playwrights involved a series of monthly meetings to discover the perimeters of the play, mutually to choose the six characters around which their plays were to be based and cast, to take part in workshops in the area with the actors, and then to depart separately to write their plays, based on the same six characters and the material unearthed in the workshop.

The playwrights had four weeks in which to write their plays. They did not communicate during this period. Director and playwrights then met, read the plays and commenced to intercut scenes and parts of scenes. The intention was a schizophrenic view of character to represent accurately the experience of six people within urban life. This afforded the scope of different developments in character and even separate responses to the same incident. It also provided the opportunity to change the gears between different parts of people's lives – in short to dispense with the usual distinction between subjective and objective reality.

It is a method which permits the fertility and richness of two imaginations, two methods of writing to countenance the same experience. Another version of collaboration.

Roland Rees
Peckham, December 1983

8

Sleeping Policemen was premiered by Foco Novo in Hemel Hempstead on 4 October, 1983, and was toured before opening at the Royal Court Theatre Upstairs on 8 November 1983, with the following cast:

DINAH HOLLOWAY	Carrie Lee Baker
CASTELLA MARTIN	Trevor Butler
PAUL STEWART	Craig Crosbie
BERT BLOGGS	Alfred Fagon
LANA MCNALLY	Mary Ellen Ray
ELIZABETH JONES	Ella Wilder

Director Roland Rees
Designer Wallace Heim
Lighting Designer Richard Johnson
Company Stage Manager Sue Darke
Deputy Stage Managers Veronica Perrifer, Paul Sanders
Publicist Judy Dobias
Poster Dan Fern
Administrator Jenny Waldman
Technical Director Theatre Upstairs Simon Byford

Many thanks for participation in the workshops to Craig Crosbie, Ella Wilder, Lou Wakefield, Gordon Case, Alex McCrindle and Brenda Fricker.

PART ONE

1

*It is Friday night and dusk is about to turn
dark. The playing area is in darkness and
silent. A pause then a loud crash of thunder
followed by a bolt of bright and fierce
lightning which lights up the stage. Another
loud crash of thunder wakes* BERT
BLOGGS, *who has been sleeping in the
middle of the playing area. He stirs, takes a
look around and struggles to his feet. He
takes a filthy hanky from his pocket and
wipes the rain from his face. He feels the
ground and looks out into the distance.*

BERT: I have unwittingly released the dog
of war . . . Peace has gone too . . . I knew I
should never have let them both free at
the same time . . .

*He bends down and picks up two empty
dog leads. He shouts and calls.*

War . . . Peace . . . War . . . War . . . War
. . . Peace, here girl . . . Where are you?

2

*The lights go down; as they come up we are
with* LANA MCNALLY, *she stands next to
a coffin, with lighted candle, cross and
picture of Jesus on top. She looks at a photo
while talking to the coffin.*

LANA: That's the church Donal, where we
were married. Such a lovely little church,
that small grey church in a field of green,
now you don't see churches like that
around here do you now . . . Quite
beautiful it is . . .

*A flash of lightning and a crack of thunder
makes her jump, she places the photo on
the coffin and picks up rosary beads
nervously. She fingers them.*

(*Looking up.*) He's angry with someone,
I hope it's not me . . . Still you'll not be
back to trouble me again . . . May your
soul rot in hell . . . I'm sorry . . . I . . . I
didn't mean it at all. Please forgive me,
I'm sorry . . . Donal . . . Donal . . . Oh
Donal . . .

3

ELIZABETH JONES *sits staring out of
her window at the thundery sky.*

ELIZABETH: I'm not mad because I see
things that somehow make sense, make
pictures, I know it's weird . . . The sky . . .
A house . . . A lampost . . . People's faces
too . . . It's, it's . . .

Another crack of thunder. A child cries.
ELIZABETH, *tense, goes to the door.*

It's all right Milroy, it's just a little rain,
don't be afraid, go back to sleep.

*She shuts the door tightly, takes a key from
her pocket and locks the front door. She
sits down and slowly pulls a wage packet
from one of her pockets and starts to
divide the money.*

4

Day. Bright light. LANA MCNALLY,
*out in her garden with a bright green
watering can.*

LANA: Lovely sunny day. Six o'clock in the
morning. Each year, in the pots, it's
flowers or vegetables I put out. Well it's
only concrete and not much, between the
neighbours' walls. If you don't put out
pots you'll have no hope of growing
much. Yes, it's Boxing Day I sit down for
a think. Come the summer what will I put
out in the pots? This year it's tomatoes.

She hesitates.

And I . . . Get out so early, so I won't be
. . . seen too much. By the neighbours.

5

Day. An electronic clock goes off. PAUL
STEWART *wanders across the stage
kicking things.*

PAUL: Where the fuck is that fucking
alarm. I mean, is this some kind of . . .
Armageddon? Ow! (*A stubbed toe.*)
Under the furry rug. How the fuck did a
digital alarm clock get from my bedside
table to under the furry rug I ask you?
Was I that pissed? I was that pissed. Jesus
Christ it's six in the morning! Right who
do I hate?

He grabs a telephone. Dialling.

Bobby Hesketh I hate. Bobby Hesketh why should a prick like you be asleep in your bloody black silk bed with some gorgeous, golden female thigh . . .

Hand over the speaker. He sniggers.

It's ringing, hee hee hee.

He leaves the phone off the hook and goes off.

6

Day. DINAH HOLLOWAY, *exhausted, ashen-faced, in a long Victorian nightdress, stumbles across the stage, gets a glass of milk, then stumbles back across the stages and goes off.*

7

Night.

ELIZABETH: Rent . . . That's for electricity . . . Gas . . . Shopping . . . That's for the telly and that's to pay the last instalment on your new but now old bike. What's left?

She turns the wage packet upside down.

Nothing . . .

She puts her hands to her face and weeps uncontrollably.

8

Night. A blackout. The lights come up and we are with PAUL STEWART *who stands in front of a mirror dressed in a gorilla suit, the head of which is in his hands. He is admiring himself and the suit and is in a fit of giggles. He is listening to some sort of classical music (perfect sound). He puts on the head and starts making monkey noises. He falls about laughing.*

PAUL: It's too much really . . .

A pause.

No, it's fine.

A loud retort of thunder takes him over to the window.

How bloody inconvenient. Poxyfied rain . . .

He checks his watch, flicks the music off by remote control, listens: he hears the electronic, digital buzzing of the alarm on his microwave oven.

PAUL: Ah dinner's ready . . . Roast bananas . . .

He laughs.

I can't . . . Of course I can.

9

Night. Another roll of thunder and flash of lightning. DINAH HOLLOWAY *is drying her wet hair with a towel, while the phone is cupped between ear and shoulder. Stacks of papers with folders are spread out. She looks totally exhausted.*

DINAH: I'm on my way to another meeting . . . Yes . . . The Sleeping Policemen . . . Trouble . . . No not really, it should be plain sailing, I'm hoping to put the machinery into . . . The what???? Grove Against Sleeping Policemen ? . . . Oh dear, thanks for warning me. I sometimes wonder if all this has anything to do with building the great new socialist world . . . Oh him, he's off at some meeting . . . We just sleep together really . . . Oh no . . . No time or energy for anything else, just as well really, since the election we seem to be growing apart politically. Enough of this pathetic individualism . . . Could you cover for me at Monday's meeting . . . I'm feeling very guilty and have to go to work . . .

Blackout.

10

Day. PAUL *runs back on tiptoe and picks up the receiver, putting his hand over the speaker.*

PAUL: He's answered! I woke him up! (*He giggles then does heavy breathing.*) Hurrr, hurrr, hurrr . . . (*Shouts.*) Have a nice day you cunt! (*He slams the receiver down.*) Well, since I'm up. (*He lifts a tape-recorder, a small, hand-sized job. He flicks it on.*) Dear diary. Up early. Peckham morning. Feel great. Er . . .

11

Day. DINAH, *in her nightdress, still groggy, crosses the stage with the glass empty.*

12

PAUL, *continuing his diary.*

PAUL: Out there, beyond my window, Peckham. Vastness. Concrete. Bashed up brick. The first rays of the sun, good old sun, touch the sleepy heads in giant tower blocks, the earlobes of the unemployed, the mad, the thick, the sluttish and the deeply unattractive, sweating on their nylon pillows. Sun on the juggernauts, parked silent in side roads, the odd smelly dog, the odd wino. Peckham the human dump, the sump where all the dirty, oily, scaggy bits collect, Peckham the – Jesus what am I doing living here?

He turns off the machine and goes off.

13

DINAH *comes on, the glass refilled with milk, under her arm a huge pile of papers.*

14

Day. BERT BLOGGS *bounds on. He has two dog leads in his hands.*

BERT: War! Peace! Where are you?

15

DINAH *drops the papers.*

DINAH: Oh sod!

She spills milk on the papers.

Now I've spilt milk on 'em!

She kneels, collecting the papers, rubbing them with her sleeve. A paper catches her eye.

Bertram Bloggs. Keeps two dogs. Calls them War and Peace. Bloody hell.

She turns a paper.

Numerous complaints by neighbours . . . Insanitary living conditions . . . Brown paper in his windows . . . Shouting at night . . . Goes through neighbours' dustbins, scattering contents, looking for old newspapers . . .

She sighs.

History, outpatient, Maudsley Hospital . . . Erratic attendance . . . Once a bookseller . . .

She shrugs and scrawls on the paper.

Liaise with health. And housing.

She flicks the paper aside. A blackout.

16

Night. The lights come up and we are with CASTELLA MARTIN *who is putting on his London Transport uniform, complete with cap and overcoat. He polishes his driver's badge and pins it to his overcoat. Loud reggae music is heard coming from upstairs.*

CASTELLA: Girl, you wan' turn dat music down. Wha' wid der tunder and dat music I cayn't hear myself t'ink.

He waits, the music stays at the same level, he shouts.

Girl, der's a woman next door wid a dead body, a corpse, an' she don't wan' 'ear no damn reggae music. Girl you 'ear me?

He waits. The music is turned down.

Dat's better, you got to have a bit of consideration for udder people, you know wha' I mean . . . Eh? We don't wan' people runnin' around sayin' black people don't got any respec' for de dead.

A pause.

An' you make sure you stay up in dat room with your books, I don't want' you goin' out in dis weader, 'cause you'll catch col' . . . Right I'm goin' to drive dat bus . . . Don't wait up for me, when I finish I might play a few game a' cards wid der boys den.

He waits for an acknowledgement of his leaving which he doesn't get. He stands for a moment lost in thought.

Fancy dem Indians beating we at cricket. I jus' cayn't believe dat. Girl, I goin' see you later right . . .

Blackout.

17.

Day. BERT BLOGGS, *two members of the* CHORUS *as his dogs.*

CHORUS: Woof!

           Warrrgh!

    Woof!

           Grrr.

BERT: Round the boundaries! Round the great human encampment of the Borough of Southwark!

CHORUS: Grrr.

           Grrr.

BERT: Like Henry the Fifth! Before the Battle of Agincourt! Tour the lines, the troops huddled over their fires, the little groups of the common man! Give them words! For the great conflagration of the day ahead!

The dogs, reluctantly.

CHORUS: Rrrr.

           Rrrr.

BERT *goes off with the dogs.*

18

Day. DINAH *over the bundle of papers.*

Milk on the files of the Borough of Southwark Social Services Committee. Milk for the cat, milk for the people . . . What a sloppy councillor I am, heigh-ho.

She picks up the papers in a messy bundle.

Right. I'll just get through these by eight o'clock.

She goes off, humming a tune.

19

Night. BERT *at large.* PAUL, *dressed in his gorilla suit, walks from his front door towards his car, a newspaper protects his head from the rain. He is about to get into his car, when squelch . . .*

PAUL: Shit!!!

BERT: Dog . . . Shit . . . Pooh . . . Cax . . . Caca . . . Big job . . . Hots . . . Turds . . . Faeces to be precise . . .

PAUL: Yes yes, I know.

PAUL is about to use the newspaper to wipe off the shit when BERT *snatches it off him, folds it neatly and put it in his pocket.*

Do you mind, that newspaper happens to belong to me . . .

BERT: Words were never meant to shelter you from the rain or wipe shit from your shoe . . .

PAUL: You can't just go around stealing other people's newspapers.

BERT: I protect words.

He offers PAUL *his handkerchief.*

Here.

PAUL: No thank you. I'll use the kerb.

He wipes his shoe on the floor.

Bloody dogs . . .

BERT: Have you seen any?

PAUL: Pardon?

BERT: Dogs . . . Two in particular?

PAUL: No I haven't. Don't you think you ought to keep them on leads?

BERT: No. They answer to the name War and Peace.

PAUL: Do they really . . . Look don't mind the suit. I'm on my way to a fancy dress . . .

BERT: What suit?

PAUL: I have to go . . .

BERT: If you see two dogs on your travels, let me know. Here's my card . . .

PAUL takes the card and reads.

PAUL: Bert Bloggs . . . Wordsmith . . . You'e got to be joking . . . There's no address . . . ?

BERT: The world is my home, Peckham in particular. I will be around . . .

PAUL: I really must be going . . .

BERT: So must I, which way are you going?

PAUL: I'm travelling by car . . .

BERT: Cars are wrong . . .

PAUL: I really don't have time to debate . . .

Before PAUL has finished saying his line BERT has disappeared.

I don't need to go to this party, I could just stand on this street . . .

20

Day. Early morning. CASTELLA MARTIN, *over the garden wall, to* LANA MCNALLY.

CASTELLA: Tomatoes.

LANA (*to herself*): Oh mercy of God.

CASTELLA: If all you got for a garden is a square of concrete, put out pots, right, right.

LANA (*to herself*): Mary Mother of God, make him go away.

CASTELLA: Make the concrete a little Eden, every square of concrete all round Peckham, a little Eden.

He laughs.

That's right.

LANA (*to herself*): His wife died. That's all I know of him. Next door. And never washed the curtains.

CASTELLA: I look out in the morning, I see tomatoes, I think, 'Those tomatoes need food'. Plants, dogs, cats, human beings, all need food. I think maybe the planet earth itself needs food. Like it's soaking up all the happiness o' the humans and the animals on its surface for nourishment. If I may give advice, give those tomatoes food.

LANA (*to herself*): Have someone die in the house and never wash the curtains? 'Tis terrible, terrible, terrible.

CASTELLA: I recommend a plastic bag of super manure from Rye Lane Woolworths.

LANA (*to herself*): Dangerous men, dangerous men, some even with dead wives, behind curtains hanging with filth.

Softly.

Help, help, help.

She scuttles off, a little bent, almost

running, the watering can held out before her.

CASTELLA *does a few dance steps.*

CASTELLA:
The warrior.

African war –
                            rior
In
            the
                            morning
Earth
            damp
                            before
The heat
            Afri –
                            can
War –
            ri –
                            or
Prints the earth
            of Africa
                            in the morning
Heal,
            side of the foot to dancing
Like an artist
            with a brush   –

He looks behind him.

Footprints on the concrete, man your socks are wet! And I put them socks out after washing them, after the late-night shift, on the bath! Hey what kind of figure are you, African warrior with wet socks in the morning?

He laughs, then springs to an exercise.

Hup! Hup! Hup!

Aside, exercising.

Castella Martin! Busman before . . . Morning split shift! Union man, shop steward, yes! He makes his way . . . To breakfast in the Criterion Café . . . Then to Peckham Bus Depot . . . In wet socks, bit damp 'cos he washed them late! 'Cos you have
            no wife
                  to wash and dry.

He closes his eyes, hit by grief.

Wash 'n' dry.
            Wash 'n' dry.
                        Wash 'n' dry.

He pauses.

Hup!

He does a handstand then goes into a forward roll and stands again. Softly . . .

Hup.

He walks out of the garden.

21

Night. ELIZABETH JONES, *dressed smartly holding a leaflet, walks up and down.* MILROY *cries.*

ELIZABETH: Milroy don't you dare drink it, put it down and get into bed. I don't know how many times I've told you to leave my perfume alone. You know very well it's not a drink . . . If you drink that you will die and you won't see Mummy or any of your friends from nursery school again, besides, it's expensive . . . Yes Mummy is very angry . . . I'll fix the wallpaper tomorrow, not much point really, it'll only fall off again the next time it rains . . . Yes you can help put it back up . . . No I'm not doing it now . . . Because I'm going out and I've got my best clothes on . . . Out, I'm going out . . . Just out . . . I don't have to tell you where I'm going . . . I'm a grown woman and you're a little boy . . . No Daddy is not coming . . . I don't know and I don't care. Just go to sleep will you . . . Milroy, I need to get out . . . If I don't I will go mad . . . No Nanny is not mad and you're not to say that in front of her or Margaret, you know what a big mouth she's got. Now come on to to sleep . . . Margaret where are you . . .

The doorbell rings. ELIZABETH *places a clenched fist to her breast and looks upward.*

22

Day. DINAH, *in her nightdress, sitting up, the papers in her lap, a ballpoint pen. She goes through the papers at great speed.*

DINAH: Housing, housing, housing. Refer, refer, refer.

Intercut with CASTELLA *who comes on in cricket whites, taking guard.*

CASTELLA: And it's the last ball of the last over, the West Indies still need four runs to win. Can they do it? Castella Martin, who has scored one hundred and twenty-one out of a score of one hundred and eighty, has been like a solid rock . . .

DINAH: 'Housing'. The great issue. The revolution? Forget it. It's damp on the walls. It's shit on the landings. It's violence in the lifts.

CASTELLA: While wickets have been tumbling all around him . . .

DINAH (*to herself*): My mother, who is a righteous cow, lives in Guildford.

CASTELLA: And in comes Kapil Dev . . .

DINAH (*to herself*): My father, who has divorced her, and is not righteous, just a bit of a shit, lives in Cheltenham . . .

CASTELLA: Kapil Dev bowls and Martin hooks . . . It's high in the air . . . Gavaskar is underneath it . . . He's caught it . . . But no . . . He's over the boundary rope . . . Six runs and the West Indies have won by one run.

DINAH, *back to the papers.*

DINAH: Housing, housing, housing. Little girl.

	Two years old.	With
Men –	an –	gitis.
Mother	Nigerian.	Single
Parent	family.	Father
Of	child	Polish.

Yes Polish. He came to the flat . . . Dog Kennel Estate . . . Drunk . . . Drink problem when he has money . . . Will drink vodka all day washed down with a sweet Martini, sometimes two bottles of Martini a day . . .

She looks up.

Jesus Christ.

She reads on.

Came to the flat, hit the mother, giving her right eye a scratched . . . (*Turns the page.*) . . . cornea and broke the child's left arm.

She pauses, looking at the paper. To herself.

Harden your heart, harden your heart.

She scribbles on the paper, quickly.

Liaise with Health Visitor and has the mother contacted Women's Action Group?

She flicks papers.

Housing. Housing.

23

BERT, *walking his dogs.*

BERT: I call one dog Peace, the other War! Peace! War! Two good words! Balance of opposites! Always, words, one against the other! No waste! No leakage!

CHORUS: Grrrrrr!

The 'dogs' run off.

BERT: Go, Peace, get him!

CHORUS: Grrrrrr!

The sound of a dog fight, off.

BERT: A word is an animal! It jumps out of your mouth! Hot and furry! Into your ear! Eats the meat of the brain! Words burrow down the ear! Words are lions, birds! Sentences are flocks, sheep, vultures, herds, charging rhinos, big cats leaping out of the undergrowth, they roam the great forests and the plains of the mind! Sh! Sh! Hear them, behind the temples of the forehead! Scratching in the sinuses!

CASTELLA MARTIN, *walking by on his way to work, stops.*

CASTELLA: Hey man.

BERT *screams.*

BERT: Arrrrrrgh!

BERT *kicks and stamps as if on insects running about his feet.*

Two words! A 'hey' and a 'man'! Beetle words! Deathwatch words!

BERT *staring at the ground appalled as* CASTELLA *speaks.*

CASTELLA: Hey man, you with those two dogs? They got sores on them, man. You better feed them up.

BERT *stamping.*

BERT: Arrrrrrrgh! Ants! Arrrrrrrrgh!

CASTELLA: Some people might get de impression dat you is mad . . .

BERT: Mad . . . I'm fucking crazy . . .

CASTELLA: Lissen ol' man . . . How come you don't smarten yourself up, put on some clean clothes and comb your hair? I know tings might be hard for you and pressure maybe reach you, but you got to have some self respec', you know wha' I mean? Tings is bad enough for black people without we giving dem somtin' to talk about.

BERT: Bats now! In my hair! Words in my hair!

He runs off, waving his arms over his head.

CASTELLA: Hey, what was that wino into, animals? Out o' the mouths of drunks, the truth o' the world. We are gods, gods and goddesses, walking out in the morning, along Rye Lane. Yes even Rye Lane can lead you to the wonder of creation.

Arms out-stretched, as if looking at a shop window.

Dickens camera and radio shop
In the sun   the cameras   like blackbirds.
Going to be a nice day!

He goes off, jauntily.

24

ELIZABETH JONES *is dreaming. Eyes closed, fast breathing.*

ELIZABETH: ·
Under   the
                      water
The houses
               the children
                              the women
Are all under
               the
                      water
Can't see them
               the sun, it's too bright
                              on the water
Wavy, wavy
               swimmy   can't see the
                                    faces

She pauses, breathing heavily.

Hold my breath
               put my head   under
Flowers down there
               orange, mauve and gold
                              gardens
'Mong the houses and the children and the women.

Breath!

She holds her breath, as long as the actress can bear. Then she lets the breath go and sits up, awake.

Elizabeth Jones! What you being a dreamer for?

She rubs her eyes.

25

ELIZABETH *is standing at the bus stop, she reads a leaflet, then puts it into her handbag. PAUL, still in his gorilla suit minus the head, comes on. ELIZABETH moves as far away as possible without seeming obvious.*

PAUL: Excuse me . . .

ELIZABETH: You talking to me . . . ?

PAUL: Doesn't appear to be anyone else around . . .

ELIZABETH: Well?

PAUL: I wonder if you could tell me where the nearest call box is . . . ?

ELIZABETH: Duffield Road . . .

PAUL: But surely Morley Road is nearer . . .

ELIZABETH: If you know why bother me . . . ?

PAUL: I do live around here, not for long I'll grant you, but Morley Road . . .

ELIZABETH: You wanna leave me alone . . . I carry a brick in this handbag . . .

PAUL: No . . . No . . . No. I can assure you that everything is perfectly all right. I'm probably the sanest person in the area, barring yourself of course, I'm on my way to a fancy dress, the car's broken down . . .

ELIZABETH: Oh sure . . .

PAUL: It's absolutely true . . . I haven't seen one black or should I say coloured cab . . . It's a bloody disgrace . . . I mean do they want the business or what? Typical of the state of this country . . .

ELIZABETH: Not much call for cabs round here . . . People can't afford . . .

PAUL: Yes . . . Yes . . . I suppose you're right. I don't actually have any money on me. Cheque book and card are in the car . . .

ELIZABETH: Stupid place to leave it.

PAUL *puts his hands up.*

PAUL: No pockets see . . .

ELIZABETH: They won't stay in your car for long . . .

PAUL: Car's locked up tight. Latest burglar alarm, they'll be quite safe . . .

ELIZABETH: You hope so . . .

PAUL: Yes . . . You reckon the 'phone box at Duffield Road is the nearest . . . ?

ELIZABETH: Yes . . .

PAUL: Is it working . . . ?

ELIZABETH: How would I know . . .

PAUL: I'm really sorry to have to ask you but do you have a 5p piece you could possibly lend me? As I've said I don't have any cash on me, I don't usually carry it around with me . . .

ELIZABETH *opens her bag and tosses him 5p.*

ELIZABETH: There, now leave me alone . . .

PAUL: What's your address . . . ?

ELIZABETH: I'm warning you . . .

PAUL: Just so that I can send the money back . . .

ELIZABETH: Keep it . . .

PAUL: It'll be no trouble . . .

ELIZABETH: I said keep it and stay away from me . . .

She puts her hand out.

Taxi!

She goes.

PAUL *stands with hand on hips.*

PAUL: Well . . . What is it with this area?

26

Day. LANA *crosses the stage, a bright, shining old-fashioned kettle in her hand.*

LANA: Have a cup of tea. Get over him . . . Saying that to me.

She stops.

Did I lock the kitchen door now? Yes I did. If he leaps over the wall he'll not get in the kitchen door. Oh but the kitchen window, did I close that?

She thinks.

Oh I better go and make sure.

She goes off.

27

Night. Banging off, on a door. LANA comes back on with postcards. The banging gets louder. She stands frozen to the spot.

LANA: I've changed the lock . . . Donal, I haven't seen you in three years . . . Please stop that banging . . . The neighbours will hear . . . Yes, yes I'll open the door, give me a chance I've misplaced the key . . .

She takes a deep breath, slowly takes the key from her pocket and unlocks the door. It is pushed open with force, she slowly walks backwards, very very frightened.

Donal, I haven't seen you in three years . . . No not really, there's some sherry, you know I don't drink . . . Yes, yes, of course I'll get it . . .

She quickly finds the bottle of sherry, she takes the cap off and places it on the table. She waits.

Have you been home . . . ? Please Donal, don't shout. The neighbours, I have to live here every day. You haven't been here in three years . . . Where have you been, what have you been doing . . . ? I surely deserve an answer.

She winces.

Ahhhhhhhhhhhhhhhh.

She holds her hands to her face and falls to the floor, she then holds her stomach, moaning as she does.

Please stop Donal . . . It hurts . . . I'm really sorry . . . I'll keep quiet I promise . . .

There follows a silence. She lies completely still for a while. She looks around. We hear the faint sound of reggae music. She struggles to her feet feeling her aches and pains.

Donal . . . Donal are you awake?

She gets no reply. She goes to the table. Puts the cap on the sherry bottle and puts it away.

28

Day. PAUL STEWART comes on and begins his toilet for the day – deodorants, sprays, talcs, very careful nail manicure and hair-doing. This continues through the following scenes.

29

Night. BERT BLOGGS is sitting down reading out loud from one of those tatty love story books, a carrier bag at his side.

BERT: Her eyelids fluttered, while her breasts heaved up and down in the emotion of the moment. As she looked at him, she realised her desire for sex was insatiable. No that's wrong.

He takes a pen from one of his pockets scribbles out a word, then writes something. He reads again.

Her eyelids fluttered, while her breasts heaved up and down in the emotion of the moment. As she looked at him, she realised her desire for peace was insatiable . . . That's better.

He does some more rewriting and then rips the page out of the book, places the book in his carrier bag and starts to rip the page carefully, making sure he puts the bits of paper in the bag. He has half an inch of the page left. He reads.

Our desire for peace is insatiable.

30

Day. LANA MCNALLY crosses the stage, the kettle still in her hand.

LANA: Oh I'm walking round the house with the kettle in my hand. I've been put out, put out, oh dear.

She stops still, as . . .

31

Night. BERT BLOGGS *neatly folds up the page from the book and puts it in his left pocket. As he gets to his feet, DINAH, with shoulder bag and files, walks by. She tries to keep on walking.* BERT *follows.*

BERT: I see you have quite a heavy load on your shoulder.

DINAH: Pardon?

BERT: And underneath your arm . . .

DINAH, *a forced smile.*

DINAH: Yes . . .

BERT *indicating the files.*

BERT: You seem to have quite a lot of words . . .

DINAH: Yes . . . Yes . . . I do . . .

BERT: Have you seen two dogs?

DINAH: No I haven't. I'm in a bit of hurry. I hope you don't mind . . .

BERT: No I don't mind. Do you have any to spare?

DINAH: Dogs?

BERT: Words! . . . Any you are not using right at this moment . . .

DINAH: I'm sorry . . . I really don't have the time . . .

BERT: You are a member of the Labour Party!

DINAH: Yes. That's right . . .

BERT: The party of the people . . .

DINAH: Yes you could say that. Look here . . .

Trying to appease, she digs in her bag and finds him a leaflet. She continues walking briskly. He still follows.

BERT: Thank you very much. I myself am a member of two political parties. The PWP and the PP double P . . .

DINAH: I must rush, I'll be late for a meeting . . .

BERT: The PWP is the Peckham War Party but my real sympathies lie with the PP double P, the Peckham Peoples Peace Party.

DINAH: Taxi!

A taxi zooms by.

BERT: You really should use London Transport, all cars should be banished from the road . . .

DINAH: Yes . . . Yes I agree . . .

BERT: Cars are wrong . . .

DINAH: Will you please leave me alone . . .

BERT: Why?

DINAH: Because I am very busy and want to get to a meeting with a clear mind . . .

BERT: A clear mind?

DINAH: That's right . . .

BERT: I see you do not want to discuss the political structure of my parties . . .

DINAH: No not right at this moment . . .

BERT: Another leaflet?

She hands him a leaflet.

DINAH: Goodbye . . .

He walks off in the other direction.

BERT: War . . . Peace . . . Where are you . . . ?

DINAH: Keep calm Dinah, this is what it's all about. Dealing with people . . .

32

Night. ELIZABETH JONES, *seven months pregnant.*

ELIZABETH: It's convenient because the father doesn't want to know.

She pats her large stomach.

It's the only way I could get a council flat . . . I don't, me wan' be myself . . . I'll talk how I want . . . I'm black mother, a West Indian . . . No I don't care . . . Me want to be by myself, do what I want when I want. I don't want to cook an' clean for you and Daddy anymore . . . I'm a woman now, d'you understand . . . Selfish? I've spent the last ten years waitin' on you han' an' foot. I want to be on my own, me an' my baby. I want somebody to love me just for me . . .

33

Day. PAUL *at his toilet.*

PAUL: Half six and no bloody morning paper! I mean what do the paper boys do round here, lie in bed all morning wanking?

He laughs.

Ha! Prince Andrew, staining the sheets with Koo Stark? It is all too sordid for words. Oh all right! I'll go round and get the bloody *Times* myself.

He continues with his toilet.

34

Day. LANA MCNALLY, *still standing there with the kettle in her hand.*

LANA: So funny to remember that when I was a girl, we'd draw water from a well. In the morning, for the tea. A well. When the water was brown my father would say 'That's water from the tinker who fell down there, in the winter'. The tinker's brown blood. We girls would move the stone and the planks from over the well and look down and say we saw the tinker's face, looking up at us, from out the water.

She removes the lid of the kettle and peers into it.

Oh what am I doing? Daydreaming. I'll be late.

She scuttles off.

35

Day. DINAH's *telephone rings.*

DINAH: I thought you took it off the hook!

She flings the papers aside and crawls to the telephone.

A holy moment, a ritual moment, the first telephone conversation of the day.

She lifts the telephone with a flourish.

(*In a cod Russian accent.*) Kremlin speaking, Tony Benn's hot-line . . . (*Out of it.*) Oh hello Carol.

. . .

Course I am coming . . . To . . . The meeting . . . Tonight. It will be the ultimate meeting! We will set the trees on fire! The wood will burn! All the nasty Tory animals will run and drown in the water of the Thames!

. . .

Perky? Really, am I?

. . .

Don't like that Carol.

. . .

I know they'll be having a meeting beforehand. But it's a farce. If the real meeting is a series of secret meetings before the meeting, I mean, what are we doing? Whatever happened to spontaneity?

. . .

Yeah, it got referred back. I'll think about it Carol.

. . .

No, I'm having a Council day.

. . .

Yeah I know, we've only got eighteen days a year off work for Council business and I've used up fifteen already *but* the work! The papers! I think they load 'em on us deliberately, cos we're yer New Model Labour Party yawn yawn puke puke . . . And the Officers want to fuck us up. Thanks for ringing Carol. I'll think about coming to the meeting before the meeting.

. . .

Nice to hear a sister's voice, first thing in the morning.

. . .

Don't let the bastards get you down. Bye love.

She puts the telephone down. She stands, singing.

La da-de da da de da, la da de-da . . .

She scoops up the papers and runs off with them, very lively.

36

Day. PAUL *is dressed*.

PAUL: Out into the brutal world! To get the bloody *Times*!

He whips out his keys and strides off, twirling them on a finger.

37

Day. PAUL, *off*.

PAUL: What we need is a grip on reality. That's the trouble with bloody Southwark. No grip on reality.

38

Night. PAUL *comes on in his gorilla suit and walks along, arms swinging. He stops, sighs, looks around. DINAH HOLLOWAY comes from the opposite direction and passes in a frenetic rush. PAUL attempts to approach her.*

PAUL: Excuse me . .

DINAH: Oh shit . . . Not again. I'm sorry but I don't have the time . . .

PAUL: No, no, no, I don't want the time . . .

DINAH: I don't mean that, I mean I'm in a hurry . . .

CASTELLA *comes on*.

PAUL: Well this won't take a minute . . .

DINAH: Yes . . . ?

PAUL: Could you please tell me where there is a 'phone box that works . . .

CASTELLA: Is this young fella bothering you lady . . . ?

PAUL: I beg your pardon?

CASTELLA: I was talkin' to the lady . . .

DINAH: There's one in Morley Road . . .

PAUL (*to* DINAH): It's not working. Just one moment please. (*To* CASTELLA:) Are you insinuating . . .

CASTELLA: I'm not insinuatin' anyting. I've just come to the defence of this young lady . . .

PAUL: Defence . . . What the hell are you talking about?

CASTELLA: Why don't you leave this poor defenceless woman alone?

DINAH: I don't see why you should presume that I am poor or defenceless . . .

CASTELLA: Oh . . . I see . . .

DINAH: I can look after myself . . .

CASTELLA: You can, can you . . .

PAUL: I'm beginning to get rather angry. If you don't mind I was in the process of asking this lady a question . . .

CASTELLA: But does this lady want to hear your question . . .

PAUL: Do you know something, I resent your attitude . . .

CASTELLA: Dressed like dat, you resent my attitude . . . ?

DINAH: Can we all just calm down . . .

PAUL: D'you mind I'm talking to this bloke here . . .

DINAH: There's no need to be rude . . .

PAUL: Rude . . . What the hell are you talking about?

CASTELLA: That is a lady you are talking to . . .

PAUL: I'm well aware of her sex, I do have eyes you know, I can see . . .

DINAH: What am I doing . . . I'm sorry but I've got a meeting to go to . . .

CASTELLA: If everything's okay . . .

PAUL: Of course everything is okay . . .

DINAH *leaves unnoticed by the two men*.

CASTELLA: Haven't you got anything better to do than frighten ladies on the streets?

PAUL: Don't be silly . . .

CASTELLA: What you tink you are doing dressed like dat?

PAUL: That's none of your business . . .

CASTELLA: I don't know what this country is coming to . . .

PAUL: This country, bloody hell, this country is England mate and as an Englishman, I am entitled to walk the streets how and when I please . . .

CASTELLA: So you tink I ain't English . . . ?

PAUL: Look . . .

CASTELLA: You want to see my passport?

PAUL: Not particularly . . .

PAUL: How did I get into this?

CASTELLA: I'm entitled to be in dis country . . . Nobody but nobody can question my right to be here.

PAUL: I don't have the faintest idea of what you are talking about. All I want to do is find a telephone box, with a telephone in it, that hasn't been vandalised.

CASTELLA: So you want to make a 'phone call?

PAUL: Yes that's right . . .

CASTELLA: An' you don't understand what I'm talkin' about?

PAUL: To put it mildly . . .

CASTELLA: Well let I tell you what you do . . .

PAUL: Yes . . . ?

CASTELLA: Go fuck yourself . . .

39

Day. It is still early morning. ELIZABETH *has dropped off to sleep again.*

ELIZABETH: Oh! Dropped off again.

Hit by a memory of the dream.

A city, under the sea. With women and children in the gardens. Fl –

She stops, listens, then calls.

Milroy?

She is dead still. Then is 'out of bed' fast.

CHORUS: Dry rot is a fungus
      That passes through the walls.

ELIZABETH: Milroy? What are you doing there?

CHORUS (*one voice*): Milroy is four years old.

ELIZABETH: Whatever it is you're doing there, don't!

MILROY (*another voice, from the* CHORUS):
Milroy's flower.
Get this flower.
Get this flower water.

ELIZABETH:
He's up to something   when
A kid is
      up to something
        you
Don't want to go
      into the room
        for a second . . .
Dead   still.

Shouts.

Milroy!

CHORUS:
Not affecting brick, dry rot
Attacks all wood, the ceiling joists
The rafters of the roof
The floorboards and the doorjambs
Crumble into dust . . .

MILROY: Wall-flower.

ELIZABETH: What you doing with that milk bottle? Milroy!

MILROY: Water my wallflower.

ELIZABETH: What? What? What you talking about?

CHORUS:
Dry-rot the tenant's nightmare
The cancer of the housing stock.

MILROY: Under my bed.

ELIZABETH: What do you mean, it's under the bed? What's under –

MILROY: Show you, come on.

ELIZABETH, *on her knees.*

ELIZABETH: Oh my God. What is that thing?

ELIZABETH, *pulling the bed aside.*

CHORUS:
Dry rot flowers, a giant mushroom
Yellow, mauve and orange
It blooms and bulges
Along the wainscot boards
Of lonely rooms . . .

ELIZABETH: Horrible thing, a

mushroom. Milroy, you eaten any of that?

MILROY: Want to water that. Make it grow.

ELIZABETH: Open your mouth!

MILROY: Maaaaaaaa!

ELIZABETH: Open it!

And the CHORUS, *the many-fluted sounds of a child in a temper tantrum.*

You got any of that in you, you got to be sick!

Fingers in his mouth.

MILROY: Maaaaaa! Maaaaaa! Maaaaaa!

She hugs him.

No it's all right love. Don't cry. No more. Look go and cry I mean play, in the kitchen.

MILROY: Maaaaaa . . .

ELIZABETH: Milroy love, please! Please! Look, take your quacking duck.

A duck.

Look, your quacker.

MILROY: Fucking quacker, fucking fucking quacker . . .

ELIZABETH *(dragging him)*: And you are going to be QUIET and play with your QUACKER. Now good boy, good boy.

MILROY: Maaaaaa . . .

ELIZABETH, *as if slamming a door.* MILROY's *cries cut off. She approaches the dry rot fungus.*

ELIZABETH: Does it smell? Or do I just think it does? What are you, in my life?

She sniffs.

Mushroom, come up in my life, don't like the look of you.

She stands.

Knife. Kitchen.

She 'goes back to the kitchen'.

MILROY: Maaaaaa!

ELIZABETH: Milroy, why is there Weetabix all over the floor?

MILROY: Quacker eat Weetabix.

ELIZABETH: You can't give a whole Weetabix to a plastic duck. Don't you know I'm not made of . . . Never mind what I'm made of. Just . . . Play.

MILROY: Maaaaaa . . .

ELIZABETH *picks up a kitchen knife, a dustpan and brush and slams the kitchen door.*

And Milroy sees . . .

The duck   on the   water

Duck   on the   sea

Milroy   on the   duck's back

Quack   quack   duck storm

Duck   down   down

And Drown!   Drown!   Drown!

ELIZABETH *kneeling, contemplating the growth.*

ELIZABETH: Cut it off. Out. Beautiful   evil   ugh.

But everything's nature.

She slices and delicately edges the fungus into the dustpan.

Oh God, should I have done that?

She pokes the floorboards with the knife.

Wood. Like Weetabix. Hey Milroy, my son, we'll have the floorboards for breakfast! They're powder . . . Watch it, Elizabeth, this could get out of hand.

She giggles.

Cut right down. Through the flats. Basement of the buildings. Down in the earth.

She tears at the floorboards.

I am not imagining the smell! This'll mean air-fresheners. Rye Lane Sainsbury's, forty-nine pee for two. Forty-nine pee for a smell . . .

A floorboard comes away, she throws it aside.

I am getting that temper. I feel that temper. Get it from my mother. Here it comes!

Wildly.

Look at the way they want us to live! Old wood! Old building! Mushrooms!

She tears up floorboards. She stares into the hole she has made. Quietly:

A forest of them. Far as the eye can see. All under the floor. Beautiful. Like the Bottom of the sea.

Silence. Then she stands quickly.

Get out of here. I'm not living with this! I'm not having this! I'm not, with this! Milroy! Milroy, come on, walk, walk, out! Out of here!

40

Day. BERT, *in a park, rummaging about.* ELIZABETH *comes on.*

ELIZABETH: Milroy, go and play.

MILROY: When I going to Granny's?

ELIZABETH: When it's time to go to Granny's we will go. Today we are up early.

MILROY: Why we up early?

ELIZABETH: Look, there's a duck.

MILROY: Not duck. Pigeon! Pigeon!

MILROY *runs and plays.*

ELIZABETH:
God. Park. Sit.
Down. Out o' there.
God. I could
Drown just one thing go wrong
Alone with a
Kid one thing I could drown.

She pauses.

Seashells they've found high
Up on mountains . . . I'm
Standing in the dirty sea
Mushrooms seaweed scum

Right up to my mouth
one wave   I will drown . . .
Stop this stop this stop this!

CASTELLA *comes on.*

CASTELLA: Now as a citizen of London, I see that. Woman with a child in a park, early in the morning'. Now that is a woman run away and walking the streets all night, 'til the dawn.

ELIZABETH:
It numbs you
numbs you   when things go wrong.

CASTELLA: No! No suitcase. Therefore not a runaway. Beaten up by a brute! Husband, locally. Run out of the home with the child.

He shakes his head.

Aie aie. Now that I hate to see.

He goes up to ELIZABETH.

That child been hit?

ELIZABETH: What?

CASTELLA: It's got a dirty mouth.

ELIZABETH: He's eaten some wood.

CASTELLA: What?

ELIZABETH: I mean Weetabix.

CASTELLA: Hit on the body?

ELIZABETH (*to herself*): Bite my tongue. I nearly asked him, 'What's mauve an' orange mushrooms?' Oh yeah, ask a man, he'll sound off whether he knows or not. And anyway, anything you say to a man he takes as sex. 'What's the time?' 'Sex to sex darlin'.'

CASTELLA: Is he a bus man?

ELIZABETH: He's a four year-old child. (*Aside:*) Is he thick?

CASTELLA: I mean the man who beat you up. (*Aside:*) She thick?

ELIZABETH: You a friend of Brian's or something?

CASTELLA: Ah. Donald.

ELIZABETH: If you are, do us a favour, piss off.

CASTELLA: Have you reported him to the police?

ELIZABETH: Why should I do that?

CASTELLA: Is he on the buses?

ELIZABETH: ?

CASTELLA: If he is a bus man, I can get him through the union. The union is a mighty human thing, large and human, with strong wings, over brothers and sisters . . .

ELIZABETH: Look, will you leave me alone? I just don't want to talk to you.

CASTELLA: Right.

A step backward.

Right.

He points at MILROY.

But wipe the child's mouth. He could have splinters if he's been chewing wood.

ELIZABETH: Oh. Thanks a lot.

CASTELLA walks away.

CASTELLA: How we divide. Divide. Shy and frightened.

He goes, shaking his head. BERT looks around, then, from a paper bag, he produces a battered book, the hard covers nearly falling off, the spine broken.

BERT: To the battleground! With the book of the day! To raise morale! Distribute the book to the needy!

MILROY: Pigeon, pigeon, pigeon.

BERT: Ah a child! Words not yet formed! Greeny, uncooked little brain, language like spaghetti, boiling in the pot! Child!

ELIZABETH *sees the encounter.*

MILROY: You smell.

BERT: Words!

He offers the book.

MILROY: You got hair comin' out your ears.

ELIZABETH: Milroy, come here, now!

MILROY: What's that?

MILROY takes the book.

BERT: Dynamite!

MILROY: What's dyna –

BERT: Bombs! Word bombs! To blast through life!

ELIZABETH *reaches them, after running.*

ELIZABETH: You leave him alone you dirty old bastard.

BERT: What d'you . . .

ELIZABETH: Get off! Go on! Get off!

MILROY: He gave me a bomb.

BERT: Book for the child, words!

ELIZABETH: Don't want your filth!

She takes the book away from MILROY and throws it away on the ground.

MILROY: Bang, bang, big bomb.

ELIZABETH: Fuck off! Go on, off!

BERT: Aaaaaaaargh!

BERT *thrashing about, ELIZABETH, startled, takes a step away.*

Words! Stones! Stoned by words! Like a leper in the Bible! Aaaaargh!

BERT *lurches away and off. The dogs cross the stage, following him.*

CHORUS: Woof woof woof
                              woof woof woof.

ELIZABETH *glances at the book. She walks by it. She turns and tries to read the title. Then she picks the book up, gingerly. She reads.*

ELIZABETH: Newnes' *Everything Within.*

She turns it over.

Well. It's a book.

She opens it. Reads at random.

'Scorch-marks on the legs'. 'Scorch-marks on the leg, due to sitting too near a fire, can be removed by gentle massage with a mixture of equal parts of linseed oil and lime water'.

She pauses, frowns, then continues. ELIZABETH *looks up.*

For cryin' out loud, what kind o' book is this?

She turns to the front page.

Table of contents. 'Thrifty home management'. 'Home hobbies'. 'The social letter-writer'. 'A dictionary of beauty culture'. 'Starting children in life' . . . Fuck me.

She flicks a page.

A family reference book. Published London and Edinburgh, 1904. Introduction . . . 'To every woman her home is her castle'.

She laughs.

I don't believe it!

She reads again.

'She wants to understand and be the mistress of such subjects as house purchase; rates and taxes; life, fire and domestic insurance; the hire purchase of goods; law; how to write a sound business letter and so on'.

She looks up.

1904? What was that? Edwardian, yeah. Houses with maids. Husbands with whiskers. Women with corsets crushin' their kidneys. And the rest of us, out on the streets with no shoes. I like history and reading about it, but it's all cruel.

She flicks pages, reads.

Chapter Ten. The home handyman.

She flicks a page.

Dry rot. Fungus with a mauve and orange bloom –

She stares at the book.

Fuckin' hell. Where you come from book? Dry rot, it's dry rot!

She reads.

Treatment . . .

ELIZABETH *is intent on the book, following it with her finger.*

41

PAUL *walking along, with a copy of* The Times. *He is flicking through the pages.*

PAUL: Bernard Levin, Bernard Levin, where are you? Bash the commies, Bernie, piss on the workers, Bernie. Give us all a grip on reality. I need my fix, Bernie.

42

The CHORUS, *that is the three actors other than* LANA, PAUL *and* CASTELLA, *pull on knitted balaclavas. They have broken into*

PAUL's *flat. They are turning it over with a great deal of violence.* LANA *stands frozen, 'in her hallway', throughout.*

CHORUS: He's been fuckin' wankin' in his bed
　　　　lovely load a gear . . .
Fuckin' navy blue sheets, fuckin' come all over 'em . . .
　　　　let's smash the fuckin' place up . . .
Load a fuckin' metal tapes . . .
　　　　Whas this fucker do fer a livin', then?
'Ere his fridge is fulla fuckin' champagne!

43

LANA: My wedding night with Donal, it was all champagne, and whiskey and Guinness too. I was so young. I had thought, there will be a room in the hotel in Limerick, and it will be pale blue, a pale blue bed and I will be a lily, a lily and what did the lily get? Love with a broken bottle, a broken bottle. When we . . . Came to the things of marriage, I did not understand his terror.

44

CHORUS: What is this gear?
　　　　It's a fuckin' CD disc!
What?
　　　　One o' them Compact Discs!
This cunt's got the lot I'm really goin'
a smash the place up!
　　　　Keep it down . . .
Fuckin' pig, let's pretty the place up . . .
　　　　Nigel's gettin' out a hand . . .
Yeah, keep it down Nigel . . .
　　　　We saw 'im go to work, what's a sweat?

45

LANA: Oh can it be him, ringing the bell? If I move, he'll see me, through the glass in the hall. But I can't see him. He'll be lying drunk before the door. Early in the morning, for all the neighbours to see! Stand still. Give him not a sign. Not a squeak.

46

CHORUS: I'm gonna crap on his fuckin'
    leather sofa!
Nigel!
    Crap all over 'is fuckin' leather
an' chrome!
We got it all?
Jus' about.
Any cash?
Not much.
    'Ere I go, 'ere, while I'm
doing this, slash 'is suits . . .
Why can't we be professional about this?
Shut up!
    What?

The CHORUS *freeze.* PAUL *approaches
his door, keys dangling from a finger,* The
Times *under his arm.*

47

LANA: He did not know what to do,
    neither did I. And the bed was not a blue
    colour it was a horrible yellow.

48

CHORUS: You put the lock on the snick?
    What?
Oh Nigel . . .
The snick!   The snick!
    I'll do it, 'fore he gets in . . .

PAUL: It's not what you do
    It's the style
        with which
                you do it.

CHORUS: Out. Now. Go.

*The thieves rush off, the video and Hi-Fi in
their arms.*

49

PAUL *enters his wrecked flat. He looks
about him. Many emotions pass through
him. Odd calm . . .*

PAUL: Ah

A pause.

A burglary.

A pause.

While I was out getting *The Times.* Just
around the corner.

A pause.

Right-ho.

50

LANA: He slept all the next day, I was
    awake but lay beside him, not daring to
    move, even for the call of nature.

51

PAUL, *wild anger, a squeaky voice.*

PAUL: I'll get you, get you, you fuckers,
    you cunts, you, you, bitch bitch bitch.
    Bitch of a fuck, a bitch bitch . . . My my
    my things! My things! My, me!

52

LANA, *very calmly.*

LANA: Lying there, thinking me, me, me
    on the first day of my married life.

53

PAUL, *fear, whirling around.*

PAUL: They still here? Oh God God God.
    Oh. Oh.

He stops.

My CD Disc player! My rainbow discs!
Oh no, they've crapped on the sofa.

He retches.

54

LANA: And I became cold. We left for
    England, to London. He said he was a
    builder, but that was a lie. And three
    weeks of getting here, he left. His
    brothers paid for the house, I think out of
    guilt. I never go back to Ireland. For the
    shame.

Low.

And now and then, there he is again. Every year or so, at the door.

She shouts.

Go away Donal!

She turns and rushes off.

55

PAUL, *wiping his mouth, blowing his nose in his fingers.*

PAUL: Right. War. It is war. War war war. I'm fucked if I'm going to be fucking liberal about this. I bet the bastards were coons, coons, fucking coons shitting all over my lovely things! War! War! War!

He looks about him.

Fucking Charles Bronson in Peckham Deathwish ha!

He collapses in tears.

Oh misery. Shrivel, shrivel.

He sniffs back tears and vomit. Then bursts into a flood of tears and goes off.

PART TWO

1

Day.

CASTELLA: Breakfast.

CHORUS: Wanna sauce love?

Sauce comin' up!

HP love?

HP comin' up!

CASTELLA: Give me egg, two eggs there, bacon, two rashers there, sausages, two sausages there, four toasts, baked beans, tea, tea!

CHORUS: With or without?

CASTELLA: With two sugars please! And gimme squidgy tomatoes, I love squidgy . . .

CHORUS: Two egg on toast!

Beans on toast!

Bacon on toast!

Put a sausage on the side there!

Two lamb chops and kidneys!

HIGH VOICE: Fuck me, who can eat lamb chop and kidneys f' breakfast?

VERY DEEP VOICE: I can, man.

HIGH VOICE: Oh yeah? Er. Good luck to y'mate.

CHORUS: Fried bread?

Fried bread?

Fried bread?

CASTELLA:
Joy of food.
Joy of life.
Food.

Knife and fork held out, staring 'at a plate'.

She died.
Oh, now I am
going
to remember
Mary's death.
Everyday
the memory
Comes
I say
let it come . . .

The CHORUS, *a soft voiced, Oxbridge* DOCTOR.

DOCTOR: Mr Castella?

CASTELLA: Martin.

DOCTOR: I'm sorry?

CASTELLA: Mr Martin. Castella Martin.

DOCTOR: Yes, forgive me, sorry. Mrs Martin's husband.

CASTELLA: Yes Doctor.

DOCTOR: Quiet word with you, you see it seems the growth in the bowel we do know about, is not the whole story.

CASTELLA: Whole story. No.

DOCTOR: There . . . is almost certainly another tumour, and the one we do have is a secondary growth.

CASTELLA: Secondary growth. You mean it grows. Growth, I can understand.

DOCTOR: So . . .

The DOCTOR's *voice to an inaudible murmur.*

CASTELLA: Take the bowel out, cut out, I understand, explore for the other tumour, yes.

DOCTOR: I think you do want to know all of what your wife is facing, Mr Martin . . .

CASTELLA *loudly.*

CASTELLA: Wish she could be, could be, could be spared!

DOCTOR: Yes. We will . . . Divert the bowel's function . . .

The DOCTOR's *voice to an inaudible whisper.*

CASTELLA: No I . . . How can she live like that? With her, you mean, into a little bag? I. No. No.

DOCTOR: Would you like a cup of tea, Mr Martin?

CASTELLA: She's not going to live.

All the CHORUS *not looking at him.*

You put all the tubes, the bags and all . . . The wonders . . . In her, she's not going to live, is she.

DOCTOR: No.

A silence. Then the CHORUS *as the café.*

CHORUS: Fried bread!

Fried bread!

A VOICE: Y'know you ring the changes . . . Bread 'n' butter to soak up the egg, day two, fried bread, day three . . . A roll 'n' butter, day four, bread w' no butter, day five toast! An' that's the workin' week done.

CASTELLA *suddenly out of his memory.*

CASTELLA: Toast! I not got toast! I'll have toast!

2

Night. DINAH *arrives at a hall, it is empty except for three rather formal lines of chairs. She spends some time creating an informal circle with the chairs, she places ashtrays and fact sheets beside every chair. She stands back to admire her work.*

DINAH: That's much better . . .

She sits down, opens a book and begins to read.

3

Night. LANA *putting on her coat. She folds the leaflet and puts it into her handbag. She walks over to the coffin.*

LANA: Goodnight.

She blows out the candle on top of the coffin and leaves.

4

Night. CASTELLA *and* ELIZABETH *arrive at the meeting.*

DINAH: Ah . . . Hello, the first to arrive.

She hands them bits of paper.

ELIZABETH: Are we, hello . . .

DINAH: Please sit down, anywhere will do . . .

CASTELLA: We met earlier this evening . . .

DINAH: Did we . . . Yes, of course we did. I'm sorry I didn't recognise you, I've had quite a lot on my mind . . .

CASTELLA: That's quite all right, you mus' be a very busy lady I can appreciate that . . .

DINAH: Yes . . . Yes . . . I am . . .

CASTELLA: Do you want help with the chairs?

He starts moving them into lines.

DINAH: Er . . . No thank you . . . I thought it would be less formal this way . . .

CASTELLA: Oh yes, I see . . .

DINAH: By the way I'm Dinah Holloway your Councilllor . . .

CASTELLA: Castella Martin.

They shake hands.

DINAH: Pleased to meet you . . .

CASTELLA: Likewise . . .

ELIZABETH: Elizabeth Jones, I've seen your picture in the local paper . . .

DINAH: Ah, yes . . . That was taken some time ago . . .

ELIZABETH: You've had your hair cut . . .

DINAH: Hmm yes that's right . . .

CASTELLA: It looks very nice . . .

DINAH: Thank you . . .

CASTELLA: An' we can sit anywhere?

DINAH: Yes . . . Please do . . .

They all sit down making sure there's the space of at least one seat separating each other. There follows an embarrassed and almost painful silence.

I am expecting quite a few more people to turn up. So I thought we'd wait until a few more arrived . . .

CASTELLA: Quite right . . .

ELIZABETH: That's fine, but we won't be finishing too late will we . . . ? I've got to get home to my babysitter, it's Friday night an' she wants to go out.

DINAH: I'm hoping we'll all be finished by ten. I need an early night . . .

CASTELLA: I'm easy, time is no problem . . .

DINAH: And you work for London . . .

CASTELLA: Transport, I drive a bus.

Twenty years, first as a conductor and then as a driver . . .

DINAH: Yes . . . Good.

She looks at her watch.

5

Night. PAUL *comes home in a raging temper. He starts tearing the gorilla suit off, then sorts out of many pairs of faded jeans a casual pair to put on.*

PAUL: Bollocking fucking bastard shit cunts . . . Piss-hole poxyfied E type jag . . . Fucking bollocks to putrified British Leyland the slagging cunts, poxyfied, pissin' fucking rain, of all the pillocks in this poxy shit hole of an area.

He picks up the 'phone while this tirade is going on. Dials a number. He speaks as cool as the proverbial cucumber.

Hi, hello . . . Sarah . . . It's Paul . . . Why am I here and not there? You won't believe what's happened to me tonight . . .

6

Night. Meanwhile back at the meeting a lot of coughing is going on. ELIZABETH *checks her watch.*

DINAH: We'll give them a few more minutes . . .

CASTELLA: That's okay by me . . .

DINAH: By this time at the last meeting we were packed out . . .

CASTELLA: Really . . .

ELIZABETH: I don't know about the last meeting . . .

DINAH: Yes . . . Well that was one of the problems I had with the last meeting. I left the leaflets at the Post Office and half of them were not delivered . . . So this time I left nothing to chance and delivered them myself. That doesn't seem to have worked either.

ELIZABETH: Perhaps the storm put the postmen off . . .

CASTELLA: That's a nationalised industry for you . . .

ELIZABETH: You work for a nationalised industry.

CASTELLA: Dat is what I'm saying, dat dey is not perfec'.

DINAH: It certainly was some storm . . .

CASTELLA: Yes it was . . .

ELIZABETH: I don't mean to be funny but d'you think anyone else will be turning up . . . ?

DINAH: Oh yes, I'm sure they will . . .

At this moment BERT enters muttering to himself. DINAH and CASTELLA try to pretend that he's not there. ELIZABETH smiles.

BERT: Great days in history gone, totally wiped out as if they never existed. If you don't know where you've been how do you know where to go . . .

ELIZABETH: Bert Bloggs . . .

DINAH: Yes . . . I've seen him around . . .

BERT catches sight of the reams of paper, grabs quite a handful. Content, he sits down. The others watch.

CASTELLA: Hey ol' man what you tink you are doin' with all dat paper?

BERT: I have use for all the words but not the paper.

CASTELLA: Der is other people to come you know . . .

DINAH: That's all right I have plenty . . .

CASTELLA: Comin' here and showing we up. I bet he doesn't even live round here . . .

ELIZABETH: He lives in my block . . .

CASTELLA: Dat man has a council flat? Boy, I really don't know what this country is coming to . . .

ELIZABETH: Did you find your dogs?

BERT: No . . .

ELIZABETH: He's all right . . .

DINAH: I think we'll wait another five minutes . . .

7

Night. LANA, dressed in her coat, with her handbag, stands silent and still.

8

Night. PAUL, still on the telephone.

PAUL: So for the last hour or so I've been walking the streets of Peck . . . Ham . . . Dressed in a gorilla suit, much to the amusement and disgust of the Peckhamites, the pillocks. So I decided to just walk home . . . Yes, yes . . . I know, poor me . . . I've got work tomorrow. Yes I've got to cut some TV commercial about toilet paper for Zambian television . . . Yes I know, isn't life a scream. Well I thought I'd dry my hair, sit back and relax and listen to some music . . . Yes . . . Right give my love to all . . . Nighty night . . . Bye.

He puts the 'phone down, gives his head a hard rub with a towel. He picks up his remote control device and presses a button. Sits and waits. Nothing happens. He presses it again, nothing happens, he starts to press frantically, he gets the same response. He gets up.

Don't tell me the compact disc has broken, please that's about all I could take tonight . . .

He goes to check his compact disc. He stands back in complete and utter shock. He rushes to other places in the room.

They can't have . . . It's impossible . . . I . . . I don't believe it . . . Oh no oh shit they've even taken the micro-wave oven . . . Why the fuck me? . . . They haven't even had the decency to wreck the place . . .

A long and loud scream.

9

Night. Meanwhile back at the meeting, BERT has his pen out and is scribbling and scratching out furiously on the paper he has taken. DINAH looks around forlornly.

CASTELLA: An' so when it's lightning I always walk with my head bowed down, 'cause it goes for the highest point, I learned dat back home, boy we had some storms back there . . .

Very quietly and shyly LANA enters the hall, she looks around, very nervous, she is about to turn to go when DINAH catches her eye.

DINAH: Come in please . . .

LANA: Oh thank you . . .

DINAH: I'm Dinah Holloway . . . The councillor . . . ?

LANA: McNally . . . Lana . . .

DINAH: Right . . . Lana . . . This is Elizabeth . . .

They shake hands.

ELIZABETH: Hello.

DINAH: Castella Martin . . .

LANA, *nervously shaking his hand.*

LANA: Hello.

CASTELLA, *somewhat reluctant to let her hand go.*

CASTELLA: We know each other, actually we live next door to each other . . . We've never really met. I think this is the first time we've talked . . .

LANA: Yes . . .

CASTELLA: I would just like to say, that I'm very sorry . . .

he finally lets go of her hand.

LANA: Thank you . . .

DINAH: Please sit down anywhere . . .

LANA *not quite sure where to sit, consciously moves or backs away from* CASTELLA. *She is about to park her bum on a chair when . . .*

BERT: The Irish, a wonderful people . . .

Which makes the nervous LANA *jump. She quickly straightens herself up and makes for a seat next to* ELIZABETH, *who smiles.* LANA *sits with relief.*

DINAH: I think what I should do is take all your names and addresses . . . And give you my address and my 'phone number . . .

10

Night.

PAUL: Bollocking fucking bastard shit cunts . . . Piss-hole poxyfied compact disc . . . Fucking bollocks to putrified fucking video recorders . . . Poxy pissin' micro-wave oven, slagging cunt burglars in this poxy shit hole of an area.

He slams the 'phone down. Starts pacing up and down. Picks up leaflet, reads.

Right . . .

11

Night. Back at the meeting DINAH *has taken a final look at her watch.*

DINAH: Right, I think it's time we got started. I don't think anybody else will be turning up.

Cough.

As there aren't that many of us, I don't think any concrete decisions are going to be able to be made, so I thought I'd just listen to your views about whether to install sleeping policemen in King's Grove. Anyone from 'The Grove Against Sleeping Policemen'?

CASTELLA: Yes I think I signed a petition for that organisation . . .

DINAH: And . . . ?

CASTELLA: And what?

ELIZABETH: Why did you sign it?

CASTELLA: That is my business . . .

DINAH: It would be helpful, if you could let us know your views . . .

CASTELLA: It would?

DINAH: Yes . . .

CASTELLA: I see . . . Well. The way I see it is that these sleeping policemen is just a start in the process, which will end with the Grove being closed down to traffic altogether and den . . . And then kids will be riding around on roller skates and skate boards, making noise throwing bricks, smashing windows . . .

ELIZABETH: D'you know how fast them cars speed down dat road?

CASTELLA: Yes . . . I'm aware of dat . . .

ELIZABETH: It's bloody dangerous, some morning, when I'm taking my kid to nursery, it takes me over ten minutes to cross, I end up being late for work . . . And I can't afford that . . .

CASTELLA: I can't afford to keep on replacing my windows.

ELIZABETH: And what happens when a kid or an old person gets knocked over . . . ?

CASTELLA: A little care is all that's needed . . .

ELIZABETH: Care . . . Them drivers act as if they own the pavement, as well as the road . . . They are the ones who don't care . . . It's about time something was bloody done . . . I don't want my kid dead or injured . . .

CASTELLA: I don't want kids shouting, screaming and damaging my property . . .

ELIZABETH: What are you talking about . . . ?

CASTELLA: When dey . . . They close down the road . . .

DINAH: Closing the road to traffic is not part of the plan, I can assure . . .

ELIZABETH: It's bumps in the road sleeping policemen . . .

CASTELLA: I don't want no . . . Bump . . . Bump . . . Boom . . . Boom . . . Bang bang outside my door, when they change gears to slow down . . . An I seen it many times, you say you ain't goin' to close the road down but you wait, I seen it happen, before you know dey'll be turning the whole of London into a play area an den let me hear anyone tell me about buses bein' late . . .

DINAH: Mrs McNally . . . ?

LANA: Yes . . .

DINAH: Anything you'd like to say about the sleeping policemen . . . ?

LANA: Who me . . . ?

DINAH: That's if you want to . . .

LANA: Well . . .

Pause.

The traffic can be awful bad . . .

ELIZABETH: That's right . . .

BERT: Has anybody thought about waking these sleeping policemen up?

CASTELLA: Just put a speed restriction up . . .

ELIZABETH: Who going to take any notice of that?

CASTELLA: I do and I'm a driver . . .

ELIZABETH: That's you. Ninety per cent don't . . . And I don't see anything wrong in having play areas for the kids . . .

CASTELLA: Nor do I, but right outside my door, I don't want my windows broken, I'll tell you dat . . .

ELIZABETH: I'd rather have a window broken than . . .

CASTELLA: You would say that because you live in a council flat, when you need any repairs, you jus' 'phone up the council and get them done free. I own my own house and never stop paying . . .

ELIZABETH: You're jokin' man, the council do repairs, don't make me laugh . . .

DINAH: We're getting a little side-tracked here, could we get back on the subject . . . ?

LANA: Excuse me . . . But 'erm . . . What about a zebra crossing . . . ?

BERT: Wildlife . . .

DINAH: I'm sorry I didn't hear, could you speak louder . . . ?

BERT (*shouts*): Wildlife!

ELIZABETH: She said, what about a zebra crossing . . .

DINAH: Good idea . . . But not possible.

CASTELLA: Why's that?

DINAH: Cost . . . With a zebra crossing you're talking about thirty or forty thousand pounds . . .

ELIZABETH: For a few black and white lines in the road?

DINAH: The road has to be dug, electrical wires run underneath . . . Labour. It costs quite a lot when everything is added up and we just don't have the money . . .

ELIZABETH: That's just an excuse, it's the same all the time . . .

DINAH: No it's not, the council finances are in a pretty hairy state . . . We have to be very careful, with the Tory Government cut backs and penalties, we as the council are in an impossible position, we can't, as we have done before, raise extra money on the rates, because we'll be penalised £1.2 million

. . . For every £1 million we over-spend. And it's not only zebra crossings that we are not going to be able to provide, but practically all services are going to be cut to the bone . . .

ELIZABETH: Yeah, anytime something needs being done there's a good excuse . . . Like a flat, no sooner that I put up wallpaper . . . Then it peels itself off again, letter after letter, phone call after 'phone call, visit after visit and nothin' has been done . . .

DINAH: I'm sorry, when the meeting's over, if you could let me have the details I could see if I couldn't speed up the repairs . . .

ELIZABETH: I don't care about the repairs now, I want to move on.

DINAH: I can sympathise . . .

ELIZABETH: I don't want sympathy, I want action, I want to move to a decent flat . . .

DINAH: Look, as a councillor, I don't have a magic wand that enables me to move people to better accommodation, I wish I did . . . I know it's awful but there is nothing I can do . . .

ELIZABETH: Then what can you do . . . ?

CASTELLA: How come you don't get the dustbin collection done more often . . . ?

DINAH: I do hold a surgery every two weeks, where subjects like this can be brought up and dealt with, but what I will say, is that you must realise where the real blame lies, it's with this Government and we have got to lobby and fight these monstrous and blatantly unfair policies . . . I'm sorry, I went on a bit there, let's get back to the point of the meeting, sleeping policemen . . .

BERT: The best policeman's a sleeping policeman . . .

PAUL *enters.*

DINAH: Do take a seat . . .

PAUL: I'll stand if you don't mind . . .

CASTELLA: Haven't I seen you somewhere before . . .

PAUL: It's quite possible . . .

DINAH: We were just about . . .

PAUL: Excuse me, are you Dinah Holloway?

DINAH: I'm sorry, yes . . . This is . . .

PAUL: No, no, I don't want to meet anyone else. You are the councillor?

DINAH: That's right . . .

PAUL: Tonight my flat was broken into, my compact disc, video . . . Micro oven . . . All stolen . . . Altogether nearly two thousand pounds worth of goods . . .

DINAH: I'm sorry . . .

CASTELLA: Back home we'd whip dem . . .

PAUL: I'd like to know what you intend doing about it . . .

DINAH: What do you expect me to do . . . ?

PAUL: You are the ward councillor, elected to serve the people of this borough, although I must say I didn't vote for you myself, I'm one of the people of this ward, I want some service . . .

DINAH: I suggest you go to the police . . .

ELIZABETH: Are you insured?

PAUL: I don't see that that is any of your business . . .

ELIZABETH: We're trying to have a meeting here . . .

PAUL: I pay my rates . . .

ELIZABETH: So do I . . .

PAUL: I expect I pay a lot more than you . . .

DINAH: I hold a surgery every other Thursday, you can . . .

PAUL: The police have been no help and as I seem to constantly read in the paper how you people want to have more control of the police, I've come to the source . . . What d'you intend to do?

DINAH: I've told you there's nothing I can do, except suggest you go to the police and inform them. So if you don't mind we're having a meeting . . .

PAUL: Oh I see, because I'm not one of your usual clientele . . .

ELIZABETH: What's that supposed to mean?

PAUL: I'm not going to take this lying down . . .

BERT: Like the sleeping policemen . . .

PAUL: Will you shut up . . .

DINAH: Now just hold on . . .

PAUL: You just hold on. I didn't work damn hard this past few years, so that some little squirts could come along and steal my belongings, it's a bloody disgrace, I don't know what sort of area it is you are running here . . . I expect if my burglars turned up here, you'd have some advice for them . . . Eh? Eh? Well I'm sick and tired of hearing about the under-bloody-privileged, it's about time that some thought was given to the interest of those who pay for the comforts of the so-called poor of this country . . .

DINAH: I should think your interests are being well looked after . . . Wouldn't you say . . . ?

PAUL: I pay enormous rate and tax bills, so I demand some action . . .

ELIZABETH: Can we get on with this meeting it's getting late . . .

CASTELLA: You should really have invested in a burglar alarm . . .

PAUL: I demand action . . .

DINAH: I really don't have time to go into this right now, but I would have thought someone with your multiple deprivations could have had the sense to have some insurance cover. I am really very sorry that your flat has been burgled but I really do have more important issues to deal with . . .

PAUL: That's what I might expect from your sort, but I'm telling you someone will pay . . .

BERT: We will all pay for our mistakes . . .

PAUL: You're a bloody fool, why don't you shut up . . . ?

ELIZABETH: Just leave him alone you . . .

PAUL: What are you his keeper . . . ?

ELIZABETH: I'll keep you in a minute . . .

CASTELLA: Now listen, you don't want to talk to the lady like dat . . .

DINAH: Will you please leave or I will be

forced to call . . .

PAUL: The police? Wouldn't do you much good, they are busy until tomorrow morning . . . It's Friday night. Someone will pay . . .

With that PAUL leaves. There follows another embarrassed silence.

DINAH: I'm sorry about that . . . Now where were we?

BERT: Trying to awaken the sleeping policemen . . .

A blackout.

12

BERT BLOGGS *in his room.*

BERT: Shore up against the world, shore up my room. Barricades of language.

He flings books against the door.

VOICE (*off*): Bert, that you? You dirty old man!

BERT: War! Peace!

CHORUS: Snuffle, snuffle.
       Snuffle, snuffle.

BERT (*shouts*): War and Peace are on the barricades!

CHORUS: I'm getting the council! Know what the council's goin' a do with you!

BERT: Silence! War and Peace are vigilant!

CHORUS: The council's gonna gas you! I've written to 'em! They'll take you away and gas you!

BERT *subsides, folding his arms, crouching.*

BERT: Midday. Always terrible, terrible. All over London, mouths, pouring out words of glue.

Glue. Glue.

Wait 'til night.

He pulls books around him.

All I got to do is wait, for the sunlight, to cross . . . That edge of paper.
Then it'll be safe.
Then they'll be silent out there.
Then no word can hurt.

Tears come to his eyes.

I used to be a fine man, with a shop, with books. Now I can't even read.

Even read.

13

BERT, *still huddled in his room. Night has fallen.*

BERT: Night. Sh! Ah. Can move again.

He stands, with difficulty.

Pubs closed! The great retreat! After the day's warfare! Now, night time! Guerrilla moves! Single syllables . . . rat-a-tat-tat-in the shadows!

He changes.

My daughter's name was Emily. Names are like colours. They mean themselves, only. Best to be a man with no memory. True poet! No past! True poet! Born a second ago! Second after second, year after year! War, Peace! Into the night!

CHORUS: Grrrrrrrrrrrrrrrrr.

He and the dogs go off.

14

DINAH, *popping into the bus depot to see* CASTELLA *on Labour Party business.*

DINAH: Is Mr Martin about?

VOICE: Office love.

DINAH: Hello Castella, got a moment?

CASTELLA: Just wait there Miss Holloway, while I see this man right here.

ANOTHER VOICE: Two minutes late out, Castella. I mean that's no fuckin' great shakes . . .

CASTELLA: Language, lady present Kevin.

ANOTHER VOICE: Oooo God. Sorry love.

DINAH *shrugs and looks around the office.*

CASTELLA: What I'll do about this one is I'll have a word with him.

ANOTHER VOICE: I mean I know it's got to go on the sheets 'cos it's on the clock,

two minutes off, but, y'know . . .

CASTELLA: We need a sense of proportion.

ANOTHER VOICE: You'll have a word.

CASTELLA: All will have a sense of proportion.

ANOTHER VOICE: Ta Castella. (*To* DINAH:) Love.

CASTELLA: Comrade. What can I do for you this morning?

DINAH: I love coming here, you know.

CASTELLA: The garage. A work-place. Not many real work-places left in Britain today.

DINAH: It's the schedules for the buses on the walls. All the routes.

CASTELLA: I think of it as a map in time, a map in time.

DINAH: You know what I'm here for. Have you made up your mind?

CASTELLA: No.

DINAH: The ward meeting's next week. Who we recommend, the GMC will be bound to take.

CASTELLA: I don't want to be a councillor.

DINAH: You love the Labour Party, Castella.

CASTELLA: Don't be patronising, Comrade Holloway.

DINAH: I am getting angry.

CASTELLA: Dialectics comrade! Cool heads! Analysis!

DINAH *pauses. Collects herself. Then, fast.*

DINAH: I'll give you analysis. A councillor in our ward has resigned. It's a put about it's illness and his bladder is bad but actually he's gone over to the SDP. The Women's Group members in the ward want a woman but the men have this pig they're pushing for. So we need a compromise. I mean, someone good. Who is not a pig. Oh God, it sounds so tacky . . . But it's not really. This is bloody Southwark. Labour in control. Of people in the Borough one in five happens to be black and one in two hapens to be a woman. But where are the black and where are the women councillors, in those proportions?

CASTELLA: I hear what you say but I don't hear what you mean.

DINAH: Just stand up and get elected Castella.

CASTELLA: Elected, elected! Hey out there, they don't know nothing 'bout us! Council? They think that's along with the police, the SS snoopers. All you good comrades getting bad bladders sitting on committees there in the big Town Hall, they don't even know you exist. I'll stand.

DINAH: Sorry?

CASTELLA: Put my name down.

DINAH: Oh.

CASTELLA: I will get elected. Election is the way.

DINAH: Good.

CASTELLA: Democracy and socialism.

DINAH: Great! I thought you were against the idea.

CASTELLA: I am. It's fucking terrible. 'Scuse my language, comrade.

Hand out. They shake.

Agitation. Education. Unity. Strength. It's nearly lunchtime, shall we have a beer?

They go off.

15

Night. Doorbell. ELIZABETH *answers it, as with* LANA *a chain held between her fists.*

CHORUS: It's little Milroy's father
        friendly
                happy
And pissed.

A bunch of red roses is thrust into ELIZABETH'*s arms.*

ELIZABETH: What's this?

BRIAN: Brian.

ELIZABETH: You're pissed.

BRIAN: And in work.

ELIZABETH: What do you want?

BRIAN: Here's forty quid.

It is thrown in and flutters down her.

ELIZABETH: You what?

BRIAN: For Milroy's bed.

ELIZABETH: I got him the bed.

BRIAN: Wi' the racin' car sideboards.

ELIZABETH: He's got the bed.

BRIAN: Let me in doll.

ELIZABETH: No.

BRIAN: I've got on the mini-cabs. I'm goin' inta partnership.

ELIZABETH: Where you thieve the money to do that?

BRIAN: Come on. Y'know what I want. Gimme it. It's so fucking cruel when you can't get what you deserve.

ELIZABETH: Thanks for the money.

BRIAN: Want me to beg for it? Eh! What's that smell in there?

ELIZABETH: Mushrooms.

BRIAN: You're not into drugs, not you.

She slams the door. Catches his hand.

My hand!

ELIZABETH, *pushing his fingers out of the door.*

Fuckin' cunt! Give me my forty quid!

ELIZABETH: I'm going to spend it. On a good set o' chisels.

BRIAN: Chisels?

ELIZABETH: For cuttin' up floorboards.

BRIAN: What the fuck are you talkin' about?

She gets the door closed.

Lizzie!

Door being thumped. ELIZABETH *walks away.*

16

The telephone rings and the lights come up. DINAH *comes on and picks up the 'phone. She stops, shocked.*

DINAH: Yes . . . This is she . . . Yeah I met

Mrs McNally last night . . . Yes . . . No, I didn't know . . . I will yes . . . I'm sure I can get in touch with her, are you a member of the family? . . . No, I'm not prying . . . This isn't some sort of joke? . . . Sean Garrity of the Dundalk Widows and Orphans Fund . . .

Shocked.

Right. OK.

She puts the telephone down very carefully.

17

LANA *sits on the park bench. A plastic ball hits her on the head and she picks it up.* ELIZABETH *runs on.*

ELIZABETH: I'm sorry . . . I'm really sorry . . . Are you okay, I'm very sorry . . .

LANA: It's all right I'm not hurt . . . A bit of shock that is all . . .

ELIZABETH (*shouts*): Milroy how many times have I told you to be careful with that ball . . . ? Milroy you come here and apologise to this woman, come on . . . Milroy I'm warning you . . .

LANA: It's all right . . . It doesn't matter . . .

ELIZABETH: He's a little sod . . . Milroy . . .

LANA: It's okay . . . Let the child play, Jesus knows there's little green for them to play on . . . Here . . .

She hands the ball to ELIZABETH *who throws it off stage to* MILROY.

ELIZABETH: Now go and play not too far and don't think I've forgotten . . . 'Cause when you get home you're going to get one beating you'll never forget . . .

LANA: He's a lovely little boy . . .

ELIZABETH: Don't you dare put that in your mouth Milroy . . .

LANA: What a charmer . . .

ELIZABETH: What a little bastard . . .

LANA: Ah come now we were all children once . . .

ELIZABETH: Seems like ages ago . . .

LANA: Go away with you but you're young . . .

ELIZABETH: Feel old . . .

LANA: Don't we all at some time in our lives . . .

ELIZABETH: All the time in my case . . .

LANA: Just wait 'til you reach my age. Oh but when I was a child, all I could see were large and green fields with nobody to bother. Healthy it was too . . . No smog or smoke. I miss those days . . .

ELIZABETH: In Ireland?

LANA: Yes . . . A long, long time ago . . .

ELIZABETH: D'you ever go back?

LANA: To Ireland . . . ? No . . .

ELIZABETH: Don't you miss it?

LANA: A bit . . . Quite a bit . . . But those are lovely houses over there. They weren't like that when I first came over, they were grey and dull like the rest of London . . .

ELIZABETH: Council houses . . . Clifton Crescent . . .

LANA: All that red brick and tall windows, you're joking . . . Council eh . . . ?

ELIZABETH: Yeah, I'd have liked to move into them but there was no chance . . . They look after their own . . .

LANA: To be sure they do . . .

DINAH *comes on, puffed out. She catches her breath.*

DINAH: Hello . . .

LANA: You want to be careful . . .

ELIZABETH: Or you'll have a heart attack . . .

DINAH: That's quite probable . . .

ELIZABETH: We were just admiring Clifton Crescent . . .

DINAH: Yes, quite beautiful isn't it? The only really decent bit of council housing in the area . . .

ELIZABETH: Yes . . . I know . . . That's why I'm not living there . . .

DINAH: Oh come on, the tenancies for those houses were snapped up before they finished renovating . . .

ELIZABETH: Excuses . . .

DINAH: Excuses . . . Yes . . . Excuses . . . I once thought, somewhat naively, that

that was what it was all about, providing cheap, practical but beautiful housing . . .

ELIZABETH: I'll tell you what, you get me one of those and I'll vote for you at the next election . . .

LANA: Me too . . .

DINAH: A dream that's all it was . . .

ELIZABETH: You dream . . . ?

DINAH: I used to . . .

LANA: I have terrible dreams . . .

DINAH: Enough of dreams . . . To get back to reality, I have put a memo in about your repairs . . .

ELIZABETH: Yeah . . . We'll see won't we . . . Milroy! I'll have to go before he starts eating the dog shit . . .

DINAH: Do come to the next meeting . . .

ELIZABETH: I will . . . Bye . . . Milroy.

LANA: You've a lovely little boy.

ELIZABETH: Oh thanks.

ELIZABETH *goes.*

DINAH: Nice evening . . .

LANA: It is that . . .

DINAH: I've been looking for you . . .

LANA, *worried.*

LANA: Why?

DINAH: Don't worry, it's all right . . . By the way I'm very sorry . . .

LANA: Sorry?

DINAH: About your husband . . .

LANA: Oh that . . .

DINAH: I've had a 'phone call from Sean . . .

LANA: Sean? He's in England . . . ? Oh dear.

DINAH: He wants to know if you need any help getting the body back to Ireland . . .

LANA: The body . . . ?

DINAH: Your husband . . . Sean was asking if he could help . . .

LANA: No he can't help. It's because of Donal that I've not been able to go back home, now he's dead he can stay here with me . . .

DINAH: I see . . .

18

Late night. DINAH *half undresses before going to bed, with yawns. A mattress on the floor, a telephone, a wine glass and a bottle of white wine. She pours a full glass and drinks it in one. She looks at it and the bottle, then at her watch. She shakes it, listens to it, sighs. She pauses. Then she pours a second glass and downs it. She puts the glass on the floor. She pauses. Then she grabs the telephone. She listens. She dangles the telephone in her fingers, from the wire. She closes her eyes.*

DINAH: One, fifteen and forty seconds. A.M. Oh, oh.

She dials again, a full number, as . . .

19

PAUL, *drunk, wandering in a park.*

PAUL: Terminally pissed! Whassa fuckin' time?

He looks.

Oh fuck.

He shouts.

I am a media pershun! I should not be adrift – ift, like sis! I! Oooo!

He falls over.

I earn fucking nineteen thousand a year, and I've actually fallen over.

Breathes a bit.

I can't go and get a bed wiv' someone for a night can I. Let on. Robbery. Shit on the sofa. Never live it down. What'll I do? Shavoy! I'll go to the fuckin' Shavoy! Fuckin' show 'em! Fuck me I'm moving to Belsize Park after this little lot.

S' a taxi. Last taxi on earth . . . Oi!

He stumbles off, waving at the taxi.

20

DINAH *on the telephone.*

DINAH: Carol!

They laugh.

. . . . . .

Terrible meeting.

. . . . . .

Yes why do men always love going so fast to deadlock?

. . . . . .

Oh yeah, always by ten o'clock. For the pub.

. . . . . .

I know I know, we are beyond talking about men. But they pulled the oldest dodge in the book tonight. Put you right down the agenda . . . Ten minutes . . . Women's shelters in the borough? Unanimous. But vote for money? Sorry! No time left. Pub. I was gobsmacked.

. . . . . .

Well, some nice things happened today. Castella saying yes. Funny old codger he is. Carol . . .

. . . . . .

Oh nothing. Night thoughts.

. . . . . .

Yeah that kind of thing. Philosophy.

. . . . . .

Yeah all tainted. Just, sometimes, it seems . . . Pinpricks. I've just put in something like an eighteen hour day, for Southwark bloody Council. Did I even score *one* pinprick?

. . . . . .

Night thoughts. See you, love.

DINAH *puts the telephone down.*

21

PAUL *lurches across the stage.*

PAUL: Bloody taxi wouldn't stop! Said I wash a drunk! Civilisation is receding from my grasp, what am I going to do?

He goes off.

22

DINAH's *flat. She is stretching and yawning. The telephone rings. She lifts the receiver.*

DINAH: Hell . . .

. . . . . .

Mrs McNally.

Hand over the speaker.

McNally, McNally, oh Christ yes . . .

. . . . . .

Your husband?

. . . . . .

Oh, a cousin on your husband's side . . .

Hand over the speaker.

It is one fifteen in the morning, what is this, what is this?

Into the speaker.

Look, Mrs McNally, are you in a 'phone box, love?

She looks at the speaker.

Ba ba ba ba ba ba ba ba you are in a 'phone box.

Into the speaker.

Mrs McNally?

She shrugs and puts the 'phone down.

They ring
                you up
                                    at night
Tell you
                of
                                    their plight
'Well this is it
                love
                                    this is it
Here we are in Peckham
                living in a pile
                                    of shit'.

I can't be out of fags, am I out of fags?

The telephone rings. It is SIMON, *drunk. He is played by one or more of the* CHORUS.

SIMON: Dinah. We're all children of the fucking middle classes . . .

CHORUS:
Shouts Simon
                Dinah's ex
                                    who has left
Cos he's
                fed up with politics
                                    and gone
S
                D
                                    P
He telephones
                from his father's vacant flat
                                    in Regent's
                                    Park.

SIMON: I love you.

DINAH: Piss off Simon.

She slams the telephone down.

I am at war with you telephone. You are a crack in the wall of my life, through which the bad weather gets in.

The telephone rings. She grabs it.

Mrs McNally?

SIMON: You can't say we broke up on sexist lines, don't give me that shit. All right I've got the fucking brass bed. I know that makes you bitter.

DINAH, *silent.*

CHORUS: On the green leather . . .

SIMON: You're so fucking cool, Di.

CHORUS: Leather of his father's writing desk . . . There is a little glass bottle with a cork, one inch high . . .

SIMON: All right! I'll put the bloody bed on the Renault roof rack and bring it over. Now.

CHORUS:
In the little bottle
            one eighth of an inch of
Cocaine.

DINAH *her hand over the speaker.*

DINAH: Sitting alone
            listening to men's voices
                        on the telephone.

She snorts a laugh.

SIMON: Di? You there?

CHORUS:
And Simon's eye
            fixes on the white
                        cocaine
Which
            to his eye begins
                        to glow
Pale blue.

SIMON (*low*): Di, Di. What price the fucking Revolution down there in Peckham tonight, if you not got a big brass bed. With me in it?

DINAH: Piss off, Simon!

SIMON (*shouting*): Who's giving you one, Di? Some fucking Labour Party hack? Licking you is he, right now . . . ?

DINAH *slams the telephone down.*
SIMON *continuing.* DINAH *pours herself another glass of wine.*

SIMON: Di? I just wanna be gentle!

Realises the telephone is dead.

Gentle?

DINAH: I am drinking too much.

She stares at the glass.

Good.

She slurps and can't drink at all.

Ha. Ha.

Then she laughs.

The trick is
            say nothing to men
                        just
Listen.
            Watch.
                        Let
Your mind
            wander,
                        to the pattern
Of the wallpaper
            or something
in nature
rain
In the hedge
            drip
                        drip.

The telephone rings, she lifts it at once.

SIMON (*all three male voices in the company*): Simon says I just wanna be gentle!

She slams the telephone down.

DINAH:
And the man
            before
                        the silent
Woman
            talks
                        talks
Chokes
            on
                        his
Vom –
            it
                        urgh!

Bad wine. Too much if you get little spiders crawling round your neck.

The telephone rings, she lifts it and is shouting.

DINAH: You bastard, why do I have to listen to your pain, your anguish, your feelings all the time . . .

LANA: I thought it was my husband come back. Outside the door. But it was his cousin. Think he'd been ringing the door off and on all day. He's one of them. I kept the chain on, but he good as told me. You're the Labour Party, you gave me a card . . .

DINAH: Yes yes . . .

LANA: . . . Miss Holloway?

A pause.

Please?

DINAH: Yes I'm here. Your husband's cousin . . .

LANA: He is in bad trouble. He wants me to help. I don't know what to do.

DINAH: One of 'them', what do you mean?

LANA: The Ra.

DINAH: What?

LANA: The Ra.

DINAH: Sorry?

LANA: The IRA.

A silence. DINAH dead still.

DINAH: Mrs McNally?

LANA: Yes?

DINAH: Go back home, you're in a call box?

LANA: Yes, I am.

DINAH: Go back home, put the chain on the door, I'm coming.

LANA: I can't go back to the house, he'll be outside waiting. I'm very frightened, Miss Holloway.

DINAH: Where is the call box?

LANA: Oh . . .

DINAH: No, I know it, at the end of your road? Big CND sign painted on it?

LANA: I think so . . .

DINAH: I'm coming. Mrs McNally?

LANA: Yes?

DINAH: Are you all right? I'm telling you, you are all right. I'm going to put the 'phone down now, stay there, right love? I'm doing it now . . .

LANA: There's a man over there, no I think I'd better go now, I'm sorry . . .

LANA *scuttles across the stage hugging herself.*

Oh
    oh
        oh.

DINAH: Mrs McNally?

She looks at the speaker.

Oh
    oh
        –

Ho –
    ly
        mother.

She replaces the receiver and stares at the telephone. She raises the glass of wine, looks at it and puts it down undrunk. She stares at the telephone.

Go on, go on.

It rings, she grabs it.

Mrs McNally . . .

The CHORUS, *like a telephone rung off.*

CHORUS: Brrrrrrrrrrrrrrrrrrr.

DINAH *holds her hand over the telephone ready to grab it.*

DINAH: If she's run off she could be anywhere. She won't go back to her house. Or will she? Come on, love, come on, oh ring . . .

It rings. DINAH lifts it in a flash.

Hell . . .

CHORUS: Brrrrrrrrrrrrrrrrrrr.

DINAH *slams the telephone down. She stares at it, edging away.*

DINAH: It is too late
    I
        can't have
    these
        thoughts . . .

She rushes at the telephone and dials.

Spiders
    spiders
        on
Your neck
    night fears
        night fears
Night . . .

She finishes dialling.

DINAH: Simon.

SIMON: Oh hi.

An idiotic pause.

Di.

DINAH: Simon . . .

SIMON: Diana.

DINAH: . . . Why did you always say the 'phone was tapped?

SIMON: Huntress.

DINAH: What?

SIMON: Diana the huntress.

DINAH: You always said this 'phone was tapped, why?

Nothing.

You're stoned. Simon, listen. Why are you sure this 'phone is tapped . . .

SIMON: Course your fucking 'phone is tapped. You signed H-Block petitions. You went on that march in Kilburn when the hunger strike was on! You went to County Hall when Ken Livingstone had the Provos over for tea and buns! Your 'phone conversations are a running sewer of all the left-wing shit going. Course the fuzz are crawling all over it. In big wellies, holding their noses 'cos of the stink. Di . . . I could still bring the bed over . . .

DINAH, *short screams into the telephone.*

DINAH:
Aaaah!
        Aaaah!
                Aaaah!

She slams the telephone down.

Rain
        leaf
                to
Leaf
        each
                drop
A
        silver
                world.

The telephone rings, she grabs it.

CHORUS: Brrrrrrrrrrrrrrrrr . . .

She smashes the telephone repeatedly, tearing all the little wires and parts to many bits. She dresses hurriedly and then goes off, as . . .

23

Night. CASTELLA *on his way home.*

CASTELLA: Split shift. Hey hey. Are the organs of the body organ-ised at all, 2.30am for split shift work?

He pulls his shoulders back. PAUL, *now dishevelled, wide-and-red-eyed lurches in fornt of him.*

PAUL: Nig nog.

CASTELLA (*very quietly*): Hey man. Confrontation is not your greatest need right now. I do believe it is sleep.

PAUL: Turn out your pockets.

CASTELLA: You want me to turn out my pockets?

PAUL: Got a balaclava . . . In your . . . Pocket, nig nog?

CASTELLA: No.

PAUL: Crapped on any fuckin' sofas lately, nig nog?

CASTELLA: I am going to walk away from here. Now. I'm telling you that.

PAUL: You're going to walk away no fucking where!

With much staggering, one knee touching the ground, PAUL *pulls an empty bottle of Glenfiddich from his clothing. He brandishes it.*

Self defence. Charles Bronson.

PAUL *lunges at* CASTELLA *who swiftly side steps and punches* PAUL *in the back of the neck.* PAUL *goes down at once and lies still.* CASTELLA, *his fists raised high.*

CASTELLA:
Rage!
        Rage!
                Rage!

He covers his face with his hands. For a few seconds he holds them there. He takes his hands away. He looks around, cautiously, then turns and sprints off the stage.

24

DINAH, *at* LANA's *door.* LANA *with the chain in her fists.*

DINAH: I went to the phone box, so . . . Thought I'd try your house . . .

LANA: Oh yes.

LANA *lets* DINAH *in quickly and closes the door.* LANA *is calm, but doesn't look at* DINAH, *keeping her eyes down.*

DINAH: Is he still . . . Hanging round the house?

LANA: He's upstairs.

A silence.

Resting, he's resting.

DINAH: Does . . .

LANA: He knows that I 'phoned you. He saw me 'phone, you see. He caught up with me and asked me who I had 'phoned.

DINAH: Yeah.

She is calm, but for quick breathing.

LANA: He only wants a short rest and some food, and what money I can help him with, then in the morning he'll go.

A pause.

But he wants you to stay here, with me until he does go. He did say to ask, if . . . If you could help with any money.

A slight pause.

DINAH: Right.

LANA: He . . . He meant, if you've got a credit card.

LANA, *now speaking very quietly.*

Could you let me have it?

DINAH: Right.

DINAH *fumbles with her bag, things fall out of it, her hands unsteady. She calms herself. An Access card.*

Here. Access card. Overdrawn actually, but . . .

LANA: Thank you Miss Holloway. I'll take it up, in a while.

DINAH: Look, shall . . . Shall I make us a cup of tea . . . ?

LANA: No, I'll do that. I'll . . . have to

polish the kettle.

LANA *goes off.*

DINAH (*low*): Oh Christ. Oh Jesus.

Oh –

She is suddenly dead still, eyes wide.

Mrs Mcnally! Mrs McNally!

LANA *comes back.* DINAH, *gushing.*

I think they listen to my 'phone, I mean I don't *know*, who *does*, but I said the 'phone box with the CND sign, at the end of your road . . . They could know I . . .

A silence. LANA *is still looking down.*

LANA: I'll tell him.

She goes off quickly.

DINAH (*to herself*):
So this . . .
　　　　is what . . .
　　　　　　　　it's like . . .
To . . .
　　　be . . .
　　　　　　afraid.

She raises her right hand and looks at it. Behind her a MAN's *Irish voice.*

MAN: If you would not turn around Miss and just walk into the parlour.

DINAH: Yes.

She walks to a corner, facing it.

MAN: I'm on my way now, if you could stay a while with Mrs McNally I would appreciate it.

A pause.

DINAH: Yes.

MAN: I'll close the door now.

With an ambiguous edge in his voice.

Thank you for your co-operation, comrade.

He goes. DINAH *stands with her face to the corner. Then* LANA *approaches her.* DINAH *turns, tears in her eyes.*

LANA: He had good news for me. My husband Donal. He said . . . I can be sure he'll never bother me again.

She looks DINAH *straight in the eyes for the first time.*

Would you like a piece of cake with your tea?

DINAH: I'm sorry, sorry . . .

LANA: We'll go to the kitchen. I'll open the window, for the night air. I don't like to open the parlour window. Passers-by.

They go off.

25

Morning. PAUL standing on a street corner. BERT walks by.

PAUL: Hey . . . You . . . Old man . . . Come here . . .

BERT *looks around.*

Yes it's you I'm talking to . . .

BERT *comes closer.*

BERT: Can I help?

PAUL: You're always hanging about the area, did you see anybody coming out of my flat, yesterday . . . Well?

BERT: Anybody . . .

PAUL: That's right . . . Right . . . ?

BERT: In particular . . . ?

PAUL: Yes you old fool, thieves, yobbos, the underprivileged carting my goods away . . .

BERT: Horses and carts . . . That's right . . .

PAUL: What are you talking about, you old fool? I'm being serious, deadly serious, d'you understand, somebody stole my belongings and somebody is going to pay . . .

BERT: We will all pay . . .

PAUL: Listen you stupid old cunt, you're the one who is going to pay . . . You . . . Stop thief . . .

BERT: Thief?

PAUL: Yes . . . You . . . You are a thief . . . You saw me going out, you knew I was not going to be there. You stole my belongings . . .

BERT: Nothing belongs to anyone, everything belongs to everyone . . .

PAUL: That's what you think you stupid old cunt . . .

He takes a cut-throat razor from under his coat.

You are going to pay.

BERT: The Ides of March . . .

PAUL *slashes BERT's neck.*

PAUL: That's for my compact disc . . . For my video . . . For the oven . . .

BERT *stands shocked and then slumps down. He puts his hand to his neck and then stares at it.*

BERT: Sticks and stones can break my bones but words will always hurt me . . .

PAUL *backs away, appalled.*

PAUL: Peckham . . . Huh . . .

He goes. A blackout.

26

CASTELLA *wipes sweat from his head and sits, LANA follows.*

LANA: Thank you very much . . . I could never have moved that by myself . . .

CASTELLA: That's what neighbours are for . . .

LANA: Would you like a cup of tea . . . ? I've sherry . . .

CASTELLA: No, tea . . . will be fine . . .

LANA: Well the kettle is on . . .

CASTELLA: No sugar please . . .

LANA: Right . . . Jus' like me . . .

The kettle whistles.

Oh dear . . . It made me jump . . .

She smiles and goes and gets tea. CASTELLA has a look around.

CASTELLA: Hmmm she keeps it clean . . .

LANA *comes on with tea things.*

LANA: Strong or weak?

CASTELLA: Not too strong . . .

LANA *hands him a cup of tea.*

LANA: Hope it's all right . . .

CASTELLA: It'll be fine thank you . . .

They sit and look at each other in silence.

LANA: I . . .

CASTELLA: It's . . . Sorry you go first . . .

LANA: No . . . It's all right . . . You say . . . ?

CASTELLA: I was just going to say, it's strange us talking like this, we've known each other nearly twenty years, this is the first time I've been in your house . . .

LANA: I was thinking the same thing.

CASTELLA: You've got a nice house . . .

LANA: Thank you . . .

CASTELLA: It's a lot different from mine . . .

LANA: Donal . . . Was a builder . . .

CASTELLA: It shows . . .

LANA: As he built up this house our marriage collapsed . . .

CASTELLA: Yes well these things happen . . .

LANA: They certainly do . . .

CASTELLA: You see back home, you have neighbours, family and friends to see you through times like these . . . Here you have to face them on your own . . .

LANA: That's right, you're so alone . . . I've never felt that I belong . . .

CASTELLA: Me nider, I'd tried to make myself feel that I belong, but I tink I was just fooling myself . . .

LANA: England . . .

CASTELLA: Cold and grey . . .

LANA: D'you ever notice, the grass in London isn't that green, back home we had the loveliest grass . . .

CASTELLA: You wan' talk about green . . . ? Boy, we have some greens back home, the leaves on the tree are so green, you'll swear somebody has painted it . . .

LANA: And the English, they're not very friendly, back home in Ireland you could say hello to a stranger, you do that here you'd probably end up dead . . . They don't talk or sing . . .

CASTELLA: What's there for the English to talk about?

LANA: Except how bad the Irish . . .

CASTELLA: Or blacks . . .

They both laugh.

LANA: Are . . .

27

Morning. BERT *crosses the stage with the dogs.*

BERT: Reveille, dogs! Ten mile trot!

CHORUS: Woof woof!

The dogs run off. BERT *hangs around, rummaging.*

28

LANA *appears timidly watering her tomatoes.*

29

PAUL, *in pyjamas, his face ashen crosses the stage with Victorian goblet and packet of Sainsbury's pineapple juice.*

30

ELIZABETH *gets to work, with a set of brand new chisels, on the floorboards. She refers to Newnes'* Everything Within.

ELIZABETH: Diseased joists must be cut out, their places taken by sound wood. Cut vertically through the joist, but make two slanting cuts . . .

She works on.

31

LANA: Greenfly now.

32

DINAH *and* CASTELLA.

DINAH: Not slept for . . . I don't know when.

CASTELLA: You stayed with Mrs McNally all night?

DINAH: Round six she said 'I've got to water the garden now'. And I left.

CASTELLA: No police turned up, no army with searchlights? They cannot tap your 'phone.

DINAH (*laughs*): No.

CASTELLA: I have told you of my escapade in the night.

DINAH: Castella, don't feel bad. All you did was knock over a racist drunk in self-defence.

CASTELLA: I did not send for the ambulance. I did not inform the police.

DINAH: You knew the police could fix you up on some kind of charge.

CASTELLA: I am a citizen but I cannot trust the authorities. That is why I wish to be a Labour Party Councillor, to play my small part in changing this country! So self-defence in the street at night is no longer a necessity!

BERT *approaches, pulling a battered paper-back book out of his bag.*

BERT: Book of the day!

CASTELLA: Mind the lady there . . .

DINAH *looks at the book.*

On your way friend.

BERT *scuttles away.*

DINAH: Oh God, look what it is. A.L.Morton's old book.

CASTELLA *takes it.*

For godsake.

She laughs.

CASTELLA: *The English Utopia.*

He opens the book gravely and raises his eyebrows.

33

PAUL *on the telephone.*

PAUL: Bobby? Bobby Hesketh? Yes it's Paul here. How's Peckham? Really great. I mean . . . Really . . . Really good. Tell you what I'm ringing for Bobby, I sort of heard on the grapevine your sister's giving up her flat in Belsize Park.

A pause.

She is.

A pause.

Yes, I would . . . Be interested. Very. Much.

A pause.

Yeah, well, you know . . . Peckham.